GARMENTS

of

GRACE

GARMENTS

of

GRACE

FROM A FIG LEAF FIX

t o

ROBES *of* RIGHTEOUSNESS

TIM CROSBY

REVIEW AND HERALD® PUBLISHING ASSOCIATION

Since 1861 | www.reviewandherald.com

This book was
Edited by Raymond H. Woolsey
Copyedited by James Hoffer
Cover designed by Trent Truman
Interior designed by Tina M. Ivany
Cover art © istockphoto.com / mammuth /confek / katyakatya
Typeset: Bembo 11/14

PRINTED IN U.S.A.

15   14   13   12   11   5   4   3   2   1

Library of Congress Cataloging-in-Publication Data

Crosby, Timothy E., 1954–
   Garments of grace : from a fig leaf fix to robes of righteousness / Tim Crosby.
      p. cm.
1. Righteousness. 2. Grace (Theology) I. Title.
   BT764.3C76 2011
   234—dc22
                              2010020527

ISBN 978-0-8280-2552-2

Contents

Chapter 1   Stand by Me 7

Chapter 2   The Test. 16

Chapter 3   How Do You Love? 22

Chapter 4   Festal Attire. 28

Chapter 5   The Robe in the Old Testament 36

Chapter 6   The Robe in the New Testament. 44

Chapter 7   Assurance? 51

Chapter 8   Taking God for Granted 59

Chapter 9   Gospel? Which Gospel? 67

Chapter 10   Dressed for the King 79

Chapter 11   Friends in High Places 88

Chapter 12   Never Give Up 99

Chapter 13   The Gleam in the Eye of God 106

CHAPTER 1

Stand by Me

F ollow me."

It was the first thing Jesus ever said to Peter (Mark 1:17).

And so Peter did.

Well, except for the time he didn't. Except for when it got too risky, when he ran away from Jesus at Pilate's judgment hall.

Before this catastrophe Jesus had invited a certain rich young ruler to give up everything and follow Him. This promising young disciple hesitated, then made the biggest mistake of his life and turned sadly away. Just afterward the other disciples felt compelled to point out that they had already done what Jesus asked the wealthy young man to do. "We've given everything for you, Lord."

Jesus affirmed their sacrifice: "You are those who have stood by me in my trials" (Luke 22:28).

Funny, that's not how I remember it.

A little later, at the trial of Jesus, the record says: "Then all the disciples deserted him and fled" (Matt 26:56).

Good friends are hard to find.

Abraham Shakespeare was a poor man, a simple man who joined a church in Florida and was baptized. Then, in 2006, tragedy struck.

He won the lottery. Abraham won 30 million dollars!

He forgot all about being saved. Who needs God now?

People who didn't know any better might have thought that winning $30 million in the Florida Lottery would have been the best thing that ever happened to Abraham Shakespeare.

At the time Shakespeare was an assistant truck driver who lived with his mother in a rural county east of Tampa. He was barely literate, had a criminal record, and was extremely generous with his newly acquired wealth.

Shakespeare discovered that he had lots of new friends now. They would gather outside his mother's home. And they all wanted money.

He had one long-time friend named Jones, who had stood by him from the beginning. Jones said Abraham told him, "I thought all these people were my friends, but then I realized all they want is just money."

Shakespeare's brother, Robert Brown, said that Shakespeare often wished he had never bought the winning ticket. "'I'd have been better off broke.' He said that to me all the time," Brown reported.

One of those new friends was Dorice Donegan "Dee Dee" Moore. Shakespeare met her in 2007, shortly after he bought his home. She told him she was interested in writing a book about his life. It didn't take her long to worm her way into his life.

Then Abraham Shakespeare vanished. Friends and family hoped he was on a beach somewhere in the Caribbean.

Dee Dee Moore's company, American Medical Professionals, bought his home for $655,000 in January 2009. In February, detectives said, she helped him open a company and gave herself the ability to sign for money. Then she withdrew $1 million. Moore told detectives Shakespeare gave her the cash as a gift. She bought a Hummer, a Corvette, and a truck, and went on vacation. The police and the Miami *Herald* did some investigating.

On Friday, January 29, 2010, detectives found the body of Abraham Shakespeare buried under a concrete slab in a rural Florida backyard. He had been gone a year. He was buried in the backyard of "Dee Dee" Moore's boyfriend's house.

Everyone needs a true friend. "Two are better than one, because they have a good return for their work: If one falls down, his friend can help him up. But pity the man who falls and has no one to help him up!" (Eccl. 4:9, 10).

No one wants to be alone.

Paul certainly didn't. Second Timothy is the last letter he ever wrote, when he was in the process of being tried before Nero the second time. First trials before Nero were dangerous enough; the second time was usually fatal. Before his death he wrote to Timothy, his son in the faith, whom he had put in charge of the churches. In the letter he mentions three times that all his friends had abandoned him.

For Demas, because he loved this world, has deserted me and has gone to Thessalonica. Crescens has gone to Galatia, and Titus to Dalmatia (2 Tim. 4:10).

I think Paul must have been hard hit when he learned about Demas. "Oh, Demas. You too? I was counting on you. I thought I could trust you!"

Paul and Luke and Demas were buddies (Col. 4:14). They worked side by side in the gospel, along with Mark and Aristarchus (Philemon 24). Demas was a disappointment. A stab in the heart. A coworker who chose the world over the people of God.

But there was one bright spot: Onesiphorus. He came in when everyone else was going out.

You know that everyone in the province of Asia has deserted me, including Phygelus and Hermogenes. May the Lord show mercy to the household of Onesiphorus, because he often refreshed me and was not ashamed of my chains. On the contrary, when he was in Rome, he searched hard for me until he found me. May the Lord grant that he will find mercy from the Lord on that day! You know very well in how many ways he helped me in Ephesus (2 Tim. 1:15–18).

But even faithful Onesiphorus wasn't around for Paul's first defense before Nero:

At my first defense, no one came to my support, but everyone deserted me. May it not be held against them (2 Tim. 4:16).

Paul knew how Jesus must have felt. Everyone deserted Him, too.

A true friend is someone who comes in when everyone else goes out. Paul could think back on a few friends like that before. There was Ananias, who had come to anoint and heal him when he thought it wasn't safe. And then there was good old Barney, always a friend, who came in when everyone else was running away:

When he [Paul] came to Jerusalem, he tried to join the disciples, but they were all afraid of him, not believing that he really was a disciple. But Barnabas took him and brought him to the apostles. He told them how Saul on his journey had seen the Lord and that the Lord had spoken to him, and how in Damascus he had preached fearlessly in the name of Jesus. So Saul stayed with them and moved about freely in Jerusalem, speaking boldly in the name of the Lord (Acts 9:26-28).

Even famous people have low times when they need a special friend. One of the all-time greats in baseball was Babe Ruth. His cannonlike bat brought in 714 home runs, a record unbroken until Hank Aaron came along. The Babe was adored by his fans. But over time age took its toll, and added pounds, and his popularity began to wane. Finally the Yankees traded him to the Braves.

In one of his last games in Cincinnati Babe Ruth was pretty down on his luck. He struck out and made several misplays that allowed the Reds to score five runs in one inning. As the Babe walked toward the dugout, chin down and dejected, there rose from the stands a storm of boos and catcalls. Fans were shaking their fists.

Then something wonderful happened. A little boy jumped over the railing, and with tears streaming down his cheeks he ran out to the great athlete. Unashamedly, he flung his arms around the Babe's legs and held on tightly. Babe Ruth scooped him up, hugged him, and set him down again. Patting him gently on the head, he took his hand and the two of them walked off the field together.

One of my church members had a father who sold cars. He sold one to me, in fact. He took two totalled Grand Cherokee Jeeps and turned them into a good-as-new car. A few years later he faced an unfair lawsuit from some shyster who had bought a car from him and didn't want to pay. His son asked me if I would come just to sit in on the trial for moral support.

On the day of the trial there was a small crowd of friends present to stand up for him, even though we played no part in the proceedings. I don't know that it made a difference in the outcome, but it made a difference to him.

Do you know how you get friends like that? By being one.

And when every human friend fails, you can always find a friend in Jesus. He is the friend that "sticks closer than a brother" (Prov. 18:24). He is one Friend that can always be counted on. After all, he paid for you, so He's not going to give you up easily. He is at least as persistent as the average person.

Most people, when they buy groceries at the supermarket, take them home. In fact, if they drive off and leave them behind, they will go back and pick them up. The average person doesn't pay for groceries and leave them sitting on the checkout counter. That would be foolish. God is not foolish. If He paid for you, He is going to go to great lengths to make sure you don't slip through His fingers. He is planning to take you home. "He who began a good work in [us] will carry it on to completion until the day of Christ Jesus" (Phil. 1:6).

A friend is someone who comes in when everyone else goes out. When we talk about justification, we're just saying that God is that kind of friend. And it's a good thing, because that's the type of friend we need. Jesus told a group of deserters, "You are the ones who have stood by me in my trials." Shortly afterward they deserted Him in His trial.

But He didn't desert them.

Jesus didn't show up after His resurrection and say, "You miserable deserters. You had your chance. I don't need friends like you. I can find a better class of disciples elsewhere."

Who could blame Him for doing that? If Jesus wanted to change the world, He picked a sorry bunch to do it with. One of them betrayed Him. When He was arrested, the rest abandoned Him and fled (Mark 14:50). Their leader denied ever knowing Him (Mark 14:66-72). The whole gang spent the weekend cowering behind locked doors for fear of the Jews (John 20:19).

But Jesus gave them another chance. And something remarkable happened.

A few weeks later, we find this motley crew boldly confronting Jesus' murderers and demanding amends. Somehow they managed, in a short time, to convince thousands of Jews of their incredible tale, including both Pharisees (Acts 15:5) and Sadducean priests (Acts 6:7). Whence this new confidence? How are we to explain the resurrection *of the disciples?* Jails could not hold them; threats could not intimidate them; flogging did not even slow them down (Acts 5). The Jewish leaders were both astonished at their sudden courage and intimidated by their miracles (Acts 4:13-22).

All because of a second chance. No doubt after many earlier second chances. But then the Holy Spirit got hold of them and the early church took off.

The point is that God pronounces us worthy while we are still unworthy. He died for those deserters, and for us, even while we are enemies:

But God demonstrates his own love for us in this: While we were still sinners, Christ died for us. Since we have now been justified by his blood, how much more shall we be saved from God's wrath through him! For if, when we were God's enemies, we were reconciled to him through the death of his Son, how much more, having been reconciled, shall we be saved through his life! (Rom. 5:8-10).

Jesus was our Friend before we deserved a friend. That's justification. *Justification is God treating us today as if we were now all that we will someday become.* It's bringing the future into the present. That's how we can be seated in heavenly places (Eph. 2:6) even when we are down in the dumps.

People need a friend when they least deserve it. Jesus is a Friend like that. And He never gives up on us as long as we never give up on Him. He has promised: "Never will I leave you; never will I forsake you" (Heb. 13:5).

Sometimes it seems that Jesus isn't there. We feel forsaken. Well, sometimes it seems the sun has left the sky too. But it's always up there.

Mary Stevenson was born November 8, 1922, in the Philadelphia suburb of Chester, Pennsylvania. She lost her mother when she was 6. So her father was forced to raise eight children by himself during the Great Depression. Mary had some hard times. And so in her early teens she wrote a poem that was inspired by the many things that had affected her young life. She began to share it with others in time of need.

She titled it "Footprints in the Sand." This is the original version, taken directly from her original handwritten copy:

One night I dreamed I was walking along the beach with the Lord.
Many scenes from my life flashed across the sky.
In each scene I noticed footprints in the sand.
Sometimes there were two sets of footprints,
other times there was one set of footprints.

This bothered me because I noticed
that during the low periods of my life,
when I was suffering from
anguish, sorrow, or defeat,
I could see only one set of footprints.

So I said to the Lord,
"You promised me, Lord,
that if I followed you,
you would walk with me always.
But I have noticed that during
the most trying periods of my life
there has been only one
set of footprints in the sand.
Why, when I needed you most,
have you not been there for me?"

The Lord replied,
"The times when you have
seen only one set of footprints in the sand
are when I carried you."

At age 16 she got into an abusive marriage. She fled with her infant son and found refuge on an Indian reservation outside of Claremore, Oklahoma. Later she lost her son and spent many years getting him back.

She remarried happily around 1950 to Basil, a man she called "the love of her life." It was at this time that she first saw "Footprints in the Sand" in print with "Author Anonymous" as the only credit. Several attorneys discouraged her from pursuing her claim to it for lack of proof. Then she fought a war with polio, and an accident almost took her husband, Basil, from her.

In January 1980 she lost her husband, Basil, in his battle with heart disease. She moved out of the home she shared with her family for over 25 years. During the move she came across a small forgotten valise filled with many of the poems she had written over the years. Among all this was a handwritten copy of "Footprints in the Sand" dated 1939 that she hadn't seen since moving into the house in 1959. She was awarded a copyright, and later her copy was authenticated as genuine by a forensic specialist, who dated it as approximately 50-plus years old. She died in 1999.

Those who stand with Jesus never stand alone.

Remember when Jesus told His disciples "You are those who have stood by me in my trials?" Well, that's how justification works. Jesus sees the best in us. As long as we stay in relationship with Him, He sees the potential in us even before we can see it. He told His deserters, in advance, "you stood by me." He called them faithful even before they really were. Eventually they became what he imputed to them.

A few nights after his great apostasy Peter went fishing. Back to the old life again. Maybe he could find security in that. Guess he wasn't cut out for a career of faith.

As the fish roiled the water and Peter was digging around in the graveyard of his regrets, the Lord showed up. The astonished Peter threw on his clothes and jumped out of the boat into the water to meet Jesus on the shore.

Somehow Peter on this night, for once, seemed rather speechless. All the speeches he had planned to apologize for his perfidy wouldn't come. He couldn't seem to get the words in order. So Jesus started the conversation. He asked him, Do you still love me, Peter? "Lord you know I do."

Then feed my sheep.

And then Jesus said the same thing again. And yet again. Three times, once for each of Peter's three denials.

And then as the fire crackled at their feet, and the waves lapped against the seashore, and the eastern sky began to disclose a bright new dawn, and hope began to grow again in Peter's heart, Jesus said, again,

"Follow me."

CHAPTER 2

The Test

What does Christianity have to offer the world? Bottom line, what product are we selling?

Salvation, right? But salvation from what? That is, to what problem is Christianity the solution?

Sin is the first answer that comes to mind. But that's not exactly right. If the main purpose of Christianity was to eliminate sin from our lives, then once we were "saved" we would become sinless. But that doesn't happen. Sin itself is not the main problem, it is only the cause of the problem.

Besides, sin can be fun. Why would anyone want to be saved from fun? If all we have to offer people is salvation from their pet indulgences, that's not a very attractive offer.

The big problem is the end result of sin. James 1:15 says the ancestor of sin is lust or desire, which gives birth to sin, which then gives birth to something really nasty: death.

From the standpoint of the happy sinner, it's not primarily the sin they want to be saved from, it's the end result: death.

By way of analogy, it's not smoking we want to be saved from, it's cancer.

Christianity is a solution to the problem of death. It tells us how to live forever. The basic offer is *eternal life* in fellowship with the Creator.

The next question that confronts us is obvious: How can we know that we have eternal life?

Now that's the most important question ever. I would not go to sleep tonight if I didn't know that I had eternal life. I wouldn't drive to work. Cars are dangerous. I wouldn't even drive home from church. Ask the pastor to take you home. And on the way ask him how you can have eternal life.

A few years ago a church member who was a genuine Christian who had led others to Christ was killed on her way home from prayer meeting at the church that I now pastor. So it is *not safe* to be unclear on this point. You might one moment be cruising down the highway after the Sabbath service asking the spouse what's for dinner, and the next moment be crushed into eternity, all dressed up in your finest clothes, but naked of that robe of righteousness, woven on the loom of heaven, that entitles you to meet your Maker.

So do you have eternal life?

I remember reading the story in an old *Adventist Review* from the 1880s of someone on her deathbed who confessed with anguish that after a life of service and Sabbath School teaching she had no assurance of her salvation.

Now that is a tragedy. And totally unnecessary. You can know whether you are saved or not, right now. This truth is stated in a famous passage from the First Epistle of John:

> Anyone who believes in the Son of God has this testimony in his heart. . . . And this is the testimony: God has given us eternal life, and this life is in his Son. He who has the Son has life; he who does not have the Son of God does not have life. I write these things to you who believe in the name of the Son of God so that you may know that you have eternal life (1 John 5:10-13).

At this point you are probably thinking, I know where this is going. But do you? You might find the rest of this chapter a bit disconcerting. Let's see how well you really understand this passage. It's time for a quiz. The questions get harder as they go along. Circle the correct answers:

1. True or false: We can know that we have eternal life.
2. True or false: Eternal life is something we earn by our good works.
3. True or false: This gift is given only to those who believe in the Son of God.

4. True or false: God gives eternal life directly to us and it resides in us.
5. True or false: John says we have this testimony in the Scriptures.
6. True or false: John gives us a behavioral test as to whether we are saved.

Here are the correct answers: 1. True, 2. False, 3. True, 4. False, 5. False, and 6. True.

Did you get the last three right? If you said True to questions four or five, you need to carefully reread the passage. The Scriptures say we have the testimony *in our hearts* if we have eternal life. That is wonderful news! The Bible cannot explicitly say whether you, Jane Doe, are saved, since your name is not written in scripture itself. You have to apply its testimony to your own case to have that assurance in your heart. And that assurance is a wonderful thing, because *why would you want to spend your entire life seeking something that you can't even know whether you have once you get it?*

But question 6 is very tricky. You may well have gotten it wrong for a very good reason: there is no behavioral test given in the passage quoted. But John has already given us the test earlier in the letter.

I have heard sermons that begin and end with this passage. But to showcase this beautiful affirmation without even mentioning what leads up to it is a mistake. It is certainly pleasing to human nature to be told, "All you need to know is this: you're saved! Isn't it wonderful!" But John is not saying that. He does say we can know we are saved, but he doesn't say *how* we can know, because he assumes we have read the rest of his letter up to this point, and he has already made that point—at least a half dozen times!

We cannot honestly cite the one passage late in 1 John that tells us *that* we may know we are saved while ignoring the many earlier passages that tell us *how* we know. It's like telling a joke and leaving off the punch line, or rather giving the punch line without the joke. It's like telling someone *that* they can get to Walmart, but not telling them *how*. Absurd!

This behavioral test must be important, because John says the same thing in many different ways so that we cannot possibly miss the point.

Anyone who claims to be in the light but hates his brother is still in the darkness. Whoever loves his brother lives in the light, and there is nothing in him to make him stumble. But whoever hates his brother is in the darkness (1 John 2:9-11).

This is how we know who the children of God are and who the children of the devil are: Anyone who does not do what is right is not a child of God; nor is anyone who does not love his brother (1 John 3:10).

We know that we have passed from death to life, because we love our brothers. Anyone who does not love remains in death. Anyone who hates his brother is a murderer, and you know that no murderer has eternal life in him (1 John 3:14, 15).

If anyone has material possessions and sees his brother in need but has no pity on him, how can the love of God be in him? Dear children, let us not love with words or tongue but with actions and in truth. This then is how we know that we belong to the truth, and how we set our hearts at rest in his presence (1 John 3:17-19).

If anyone says, "I love God," yet hates his brother, he is a liar. For anyone who does not love his brother, whom he has seen, cannot love God, whom he has not seen. And he has given us this command: Whoever loves God must also love his brother (1 John 4:20, 21).

John was probably a teenager when Jesus called him. He started out as a young hothead, a Son of Thunder. But along the way something happened to John as he walked with Jesus and absorbed His gentle spirit of humility and patience. As he suffered persecution and hardship, John's fierceness began to melt, until he became a loving and lovable Christian. Young John Thunder became Old John Tender. We know this from his first Epistle. The letter is a symphony of tender love. The word "love" appears in almost every verse.

1 Corinthians 13 is usually regarded as the love chapter in the Bible. But that chapter uses the word love only 8 times. 1 John 4 uses it 21 times. John is stuck like a broken record on this theme. The way we know we are saved is if we love our brother. There is no need for subtle exegesis here; the mean-

ing is crystal clear. John says in 1 John 5:13 *that* we may know we have eternal life only after he has repeatedly said *how* we may know. And the test is not some forensic declaration. It's not abstract belief. It is not a loving feeling. It is loving behavior. God's children all bear the birthmark, and that birthmark is love.

> Dear friends, let us love one another, for love comes from God. Everyone who loves has been born of God and knows God. Whoever does not love does not know God, because God is love (1 John 4:7, 8).

> No one has ever seen God; but if we love one another, God lives in us and his love is made complete in us (1 John 4:12).

> Of course, this is all in the context of belief in Jesus. That's fundamental.

Everyone reading this book wants God to live in them. Love one another, says John, and you will discover God living in you. And if we have God living in us, then we have nothing to fear from the future, do we!

A lot of Christians worry about the day of judgment. How am I going to stand on that day? How can I have confidence in the judgment? Well, John has an answer to that question too:

> And so we know and rely on the love God has for us. God is love. Whoever lives in love lives in God, and God in him. In this way, love is made complete among us so that we will have confidence on the day of judgment, because in this world we are like him (1 John 4:16, 17).

What is the secret to confidence on the day of judgment? Well, just love people selflessly, like Jesus did, and you'll have it.

Paul says something similar in 1 Timothy 3:13: "Those who have served well gain an excellent standing and great assurance in their faith in Christ Jesus." Assurance comes through loving service to others.

Love is the requirement for heaven. Heaven would not be heaven if some people there didn't love other people there. So God has given us a training period here on earth, kind of a boot camp for heaven. And if we live in love down here, then our churches and our homes and even our workplaces can become a little heaven on earth.

Frank Belden wrote a song about love that many of us learned as a child.

'Tis love that makes us happy,
'Tis love that smooths the way;
It helps us mind, it makes us kind
To others every day.

God is love; we're His little children.
God is love; we would be like Him.
'Tis love that makes us happy,
'Tis love that smooths the way;
It helps us "mind," it makes us kind
To others every day.

And when this life is over,
And we are called above
Our song shall be, eternally,
Of Jesus and His love.

CHAPTER 3

How Do You Love?

Practically speaking, what does it mean to love our brothers? Is it holding a warm feeling in the heart toward them, or is it doing something to create warm feelings in their heart? I would suggest that it does not matter how you feel about them at all. You can love people you dislike. Love is a principle, and if you act on the principle, the feelings will come. Or as C. S. Lewis put it: "Do not waste time bothering whether you 'love' your neighbor; act as if you did. As soon as we do this we find one of the great secrets. When you are behaving as if you loved someone, you will presently come to love him."

A friend of mine once told me about an experiment in loving. She couldn't stand a certain woman who was a member of her church. This woman was always putting on airs of superiority. But one day my friend decided to ignore her feelings and take one small step toward friendship, suspecting that the object of her revulsion rarely received love from others. She finally was able to come up with one thing she admired about this woman—the way she raised her daughter. One day in the church foyer she complimented her on that, reaching out to touch her affectionately on the shoulder. At that moment, she said, her feelings changed, and the two soon became fast friends.

One of the most enduring stories about the power of redeeming love is Victor Hugo's story *Les Miserables.* At the center of the story is an escaped convict, Jean Valjean, who was imprisoned for 20 years because he stole a loaf of bread. He finds mercy and hospitality in the home of a bishop. But in that home he falls back into old habit patterns and steals some of the bishop's silver and disappears into the night.

A constable stops him, and he tries to lie his way out of trouble: The silver was a gift, he says. The constable takes him back to the bishop and Jean Valjean waits to hear the words that will return him to prison until he dies. Nothing in his life prepared him for what he is about to hear.

"Of course this silver was my gift," says the bishop. "But wait—you forgot the most valuable part. You forgot to take the silver candlesticks."

Instead of the condemnation he deserves, Valjean is blindsided by grace. One moment he faces poverty and prison, the next freedom and abundance.

Before Valjean leaves, the bishop says to him, "You must never forget this moment. Your soul and your life have been bought back. You are not your own. From now on, you belong to God."

And because of grace, Jean Valjean's life becomes an act of love. He honors the promise he gave to a dying prostitute: he devotes himself to raising her child, whose name is Cosette. Later he faces peril to save the man who loves Cosette, even though he knows it may mean living life alone.

In the end Valjean, the convict, is able to love. He comes to see what is expressed so beautifully in the musical Les Miz: "To love another person is to see the face of God."

Now go and love like that!

The best definition of love I have ever seen is this: love exists when the welfare (satisfaction, security, happiness) of the beloved is more important than one's own welfare.

John's definition is very similar:

> This is how we know what love is: Jesus Christ laid down his life for us. And we ought to lay down our lives for our brothers. If anyone has material possessions and sees his brother in need but has no pity on him, how can the love of God be in him? (1 John 3:16, 17).

The first part of this verse may seem like a tall order. Maybe laying down your life for someone else seems a bit beyond what you are capable of right now. But God will not call you to face that test until you are ready for it. In a moment we'll see how John faced it. For now just concentrate on the second half of the verse. Everyone can share with someone in need. If we have the means to meet our brother's need and have no pity on him, then we cannot meet the love test.

The early church took this very seriously. "All the believers were together and had everything in common. Selling their possessions and goods, they gave to anyone as he had need" (Acts 2:44, 45). "No one claimed that any of his possessions was his own, but they shared everything they had" (Acts 4:32). Around the end of the first century the *Didache* (4.8) prescribed: "You shall not turn away from someone in need, but shall share everything with your brother, and not claim that anything is your own." Eusebius wrote that many of the leading disciples in the first half of the second century "first fulfilled the Savior's command and distributed their property to the needy, then, starting on their journey, they took up the work of evangelists and were zealous to preach to all who had not yet heard the word of the faith" (Eusebius, *Hist.* 3.37.2). About 160 the critic Lucian described "these imbeciles," the Christians, as "disdaining things terrestrial, and holding these as belonging to all in common" (Lucian, *Peregrinus Proteus*). A generation later Tertullian declared, "The family possessions which generally destroy brotherhood among you, create fraternal bonds among us. One in mind and soul, we do not hesitate to share our earthly goods with one another. All things except our wives are common among us" (Tertullian, *Apologeticus,* 39.11).

By the end of the fourth century St. Chrysostom was bemoaning the lapse of the church: "It is not for lack of miracles that the church is staid, it is because we have forsaken the angelic life of Pentecost and fallen back on private property. If we lived as they did, with all things common, we should soon convert the whole world, with no need of miracles at all" (Chrysostom, *Homily* 25).

We have some work to do to reach the standard set by the early church. None of us love as perfectly as we ought. But the love test is not an impossibly high standard. It is a practical test that every Christian can pass. It is a mistake to assume that every act of love must be perfect or it is worthless. God will perfect our love in His own good time. We look forward, not back.

We may be dismayed as we look back on a rather spotty record in the love department. We did not at all times act in a fully loving way.

That does not mean we fail the test. Loving just means not turning our back when our brother is in need. John doesn't say we have to love *perfectly*. Human beings don't do anything perfectly.

Perfectionism is the enemy here. We are not saved on the condition of perfect behavior. If we love someone perfectly, then one might argue that we should be there for them all the time to meet any need they might ever have. But that is not even possible within one's immediate family.

No one is saved on the condition of perfect behavior. Jesus said that a tree is known by its fruit (Luke 6:44). If you find apples, then it is an apple tree. If you find little round prickly balls, then it is a sweetgum. If you find cones, it's a conifer. If you find lemons, it's a lemon tree.

An apple tree does not bear thorns. But neither does it always bear perfect apples. What if some of the apples are wormy? Does that mean that this so-called apple tree is really a conifer? Or a lemon tree?

Or is it still an apple tree—with potential?

God asks us to bear fruit for Him. The fruit of the Spirit is love, joy, peace, long-suffering, and so forth (Gal. 5:22). No one bears perfect fruit all the time. Maybe a few of the apples on that tree have rotten spots. But it's still an apple tree. And as for those wormy apples, well, God is good at tree surgery.

Les Miserables is a fable. Here then is a much better tale that is almost certainly true. This amazing story demonstrates just what John meant when he wrote "perfect love drives out fear" (1 John 4:18), and "greater love has no one than this, that he lay down his life for his friends" (John 15:13). Clement of Alexandria recorded this story less than a hundred years after it happened in his book *What Rich Man Can Be Saved?* (chapter 42). There is a good chance these events took place in Smyrna. The reason Clement did not name the city was probably to avoid embarrassing Bishop Polycarp, who was 30-something at the time of the story but who was martyred more than 50 years later, and by the time Clement wrote, Polycarp and his writings were revered in the church. This thrilling story, also found in Eusebius' *Ecclesiastical History* 3.23, is one of the Christianity's best-kept secrets. The narrative below is a close paraphrase after consulting several translations, becoming quite exact where John's speech is quoted.

After the death of the emperor Domitian, who had exiled John to the island of Patmos, John was allowed to return to Ephesus. From this headquarters he traveled to various neighboring Gentile territories to appoint bishops and ordain new ministers, under the guidance of the Holy Spirit.

At one nearby city he spied a handsome youth of powerful physique and ardent temperament. He told the bishop, "I commit this young man to your diligent care in the presence of the church and with Christ as witness." After the bishop accepted the charge, John returned to Ephesus.

So the bishop took the youth home with him, trained him, loved him, and finally baptized him. But then he relaxed his vigilance.

Somehow the young man fell in with the wrong crowd. At first the gang enticed him by showing him a good time, paying his way into expensive places of entertainment. Then they took him out with them at night on robberies. Finally they made him an accomplice in more serious offenses. He fell headlong into a life of crime and renounced his salvation. Being a natural leader, he became a chief of a band of robbers, the most violent, most bloody, most cruel of them all.

Eventually the church sent for John over some ecclesiastical matter. After setting everything in order, he said, "Come now, Bishop, restore the deposit which both I and Christ committed to you in the presence of the church over which you preside."

At first the bishop was confused, thinking that John was accusing him of embezzling money. He didn't know what to think. He knew John wouldn't make things up, and he knew he wasn't a thief. Then John said, "I demand from you the soul of that young man who was your brother."

The bishop groaned deeply and burst into tears. "He is dead," he said.

"How did he die," said John?

"He is dead to God, for he turned out to be wicked and dissolute, and became a robber. And now, instead of the church, he haunts the mountain with a band of men like him."

The apostle was so upset at this that he tore his clothes, struck himself on the head, and lamented, "A fine guard I left for a brother's soul! Now bring me a horse, and let someone show me the way."

So he rode away from the church just as he was, and soon found himself in the bandits' territory. The outlaws had posted lookouts, who saw him and took him prisoner. He made no attempt to flee, but said, "take me to your leader. That's what I came for."

The captain was armed and waiting. As the old man approached, something about him seemed familiar. Suddenly he recognized John, and turned in shame to flee.

The dignified old apostle forgot his age, and pursued him with all his might. He cried out, "Why, my son, do you flee from me, your own father, unarmed, aged? Have pity, my son; fear not; you still have hope of life. I will intercede with Christ for you. If necessary, I will cheerfully suffer death for you as the Lord did for us. I will give my life for yours. Stand still and believe that Christ has sent me."

At this the young man stopped and looked down; then threw down his weapons and began to tremble and weep bitterly. As the old man approached, the youth embraced him, confessing his sins and baptizing himself a second time with his tears, but concealing his right hand (the hand that had committed murder).

The apostle assured him on oath that he would find forgiveness with the Savior. He pled with him upon his knees, and kissed his right hand itself as if it were now purified by repentance, and so led him back to the church.

There he interceded constantly for the youth with much prayer, and struggled with him through continual fasts, and calmed his fears.

John did not leave until he had restored him to the church, giving us a shining example of true repentance and a wonderful proof of regeneration, a trophy of the resurrection for which we hope.

CHAPTER 4

Festal Attire

There is a saying "Clothes make the man." Ancient peoples often believed this quite literally. Clothes were regarded as an extension of one's self. It was believed, for example, that if you merely touched the robe of a holy man, you could be healed, for the robe itself contained his virtue.

This idea that "you are what you wear" is still around. John Malloy's bestseller, *Dress for Success*, which originally came out in 1988, is still around in a revised edition. I haven't read the revised edition, but Malloy claimed in the original edition that pinstripes were in but short sleeves were out, along with other assorted dictums about how to conform to the executive image.

There is a certain fancy restaurant in New York City which will not let anyone in without a tie. Some years ago, the story goes, even Burt Reynolds tried to get in but was refused because he didn't have on a tie. This same restaurant gladly offers to provide its patrons with a tie if they don't have one. I guess Burt just felt he was special—he didn't need a tie. They threw him out.

Well, heaven is like that too. Without the right clothes you can't get in. There is an exacting protocol to which everyone is expected to conform, and there are no exceptions. And heaven supplies the clothes. You can't eat in heavenly places without the right clothes. You can't get in without the robe.

In Jesus' day the custom was that when the invitations to some great feast, such as a wedding feast, were sent out, the time was not stated, and when everything was ready the servants were sent out with a final summons to tell the guests to come.

Now in ancient times they really knew how to feast! What else did they have to do? No television, no Internet. No virtual reality. The biggest events of their year were feasts. Some royal feasts could last more than a month. Jewish feasts more commonly lasted seven days, and the guests were expected to stay the whole time. It was an insult to the host to leave early. But an entire week was a major commitment of time to be away from the farm or the fishing or whatever your occupation might be. Perhaps that is why the invitation to the feast in Luke 14:16-24 met with so many excuses:

> Jesus replied: "A certain man was preparing a great banquet and invited many guests. At the time of the banquet he sent his servant to tell those who had been invited, 'Come, for everything is now ready.' But they all alike began to make excuses. The first said, 'I have just bought a field, and I must go and see it. Please excuse me.' Another said, 'I have just bought five yoke of oxen, and I'm on my way to try them out. Please excuse me.' Still another said, 'I just got married, so I can't come.'"

As the parable continues, the feast-giver gets upset over the affront to his generosity. He revokes the invitations of the respectable people, and sends his messengers across the tracks over to the low-rent district. And there the parable ends. But Matthew adds a long appendix to this parable.

In the version of the parable found in Matthew 22 the too-busy-with-my-own-business crowd don't even bother to make excuses. They just ignore the messengers. So the landowner offers his hospitality to another class of people who are more likely to feel honored by such an invitation. But this creates a problem. What to do about clothes? These people would lack suitable attire for such high society.

It is possible that Jesus is borrowing and altering a rabbinic parable that may have been familiar to His audience. That parable goes like this: There was a king who invited his guests to a feast, without telling them the exact date and time; but he did tell them that they must wash, and anoint, and clothe themselves that they might be ready when the summons came.

The wise prepared themselves at once, and took their places waiting at the palace door, for they believed that in a palace a feast could be prepared so quickly that there would be no long warning. The foolish believed that it would take a long time to make the necessary preparations and that they would have plenty of time. So they went, the mason to his lime, the potter to his clay, the smith to his furnace, the fuller to his bleaching-ground, and went on with their work.

Then, suddenly, the summons to the feast came without any warning. The wise were ready to sit down, and the king rejoiced over them, and they ate and drank. but those who had not arrayed themselves in their wedding garments had to stand outside, sad and hungry, and look on at the joy that they had lost.

You can see that Christ's parable of the wise and foolish virgins may also owe something to this rabbinic parable. Of course, we cannot be certain the rabbinic parable is older, since written rabbinic sources are in fact later than the Gospels, although the stories in the texts usually go back to much earlier times. It is possible the rabbis were listening when Jesus told His parables. But most scholars consider it more likely that the rabbinic parable is older.

One of the greatest of human failings, and one of the least discussed—something I consider perhaps my own worst fault—is the problem of letting opportunity pass. When we are young we regret what we have done. When we are old we regret what we might have done but neglected to do. How many of us could be wealthy—whether in friends, family, disciples, influence, money, health, or time—if we had only leaped when opportunity knocked. Jesus came preaching the coming kingdom of God, the greatest opportunity of all time. We must never let our plans preempt the kingdom. Nothing is more important than answering God's call, whatever form it may take, when it comes.

When the feast was ready, and the final invitation to the kingdom was sent out by the King's Son Himself, God's chosen people refused to come. The sad result of their refusal was the ultimate destruction of their city by Roman fire in A.D. 70, which Jesus predicted in verse 7 of this parable.

But the feast must go on. So the king sent his servants to call a different sort of folks—that is, the Gentiles.

> Then he said to his servants, "The wedding banquet is ready, but those I invited did not deserve to come. Go to the street corners and invite to the banquet anyone you find." So the servants went out into the streets and

gathered all the people they could find, both good and bad, and the wedding hall was filled with guests (Matt. 22:8-10).

Note first that the invitation was one of grace. The "good" folks proved themselves unworthy by refusing to come, so the generous master of the feast sent his servants over to the ghetto, the high-crime district, whose denizens would normally of themselves have no hope of ever being invited to such a feast. They were not socially acceptable. They didn't have any good clothes. Some of them hadn't had a bath in a good while—and this in a time when even clean people didn't bathe very often. Some of these folks had done nothing to earn such a privilege; and I imagine they were quite excited by an invitation that did not discriminate between parties but was open to all, "good and bad."

But the king could not allow people who were dressed like these folks in his spotless dining room. After all, they would feel ashamed and out of place. The king wanted his guests to feel that they belonged. There was only one thing to do—he had to provide the clothes. Which he did, free of charge.

The king did everything that he could do. He did the advertising, he provided the feast, and he even provided the clothes. What more could he do? The only thing he didn't do was dress them and eat for them.

What happens next is chilling:

> But when the king came in to see the guests, he noticed a man there who was not wearing wedding clothes. "Friend," he asked, "how did you get in here without wedding clothes?" The man was speechless. Then the king told the attendants, "Tie him hand and foot, and throw him outside, into the darkness, where there will be weeping and gnashing of teeth." For many are invited, but few are chosen (Matt. 22:11-14).

Here is what's so chilling. Jesus called him "friend." That was the term He reserved for His closest associates, the inner circle of the twelve (cf. Matt. 26:50; Luke 12:4; John 15:13-15; 21:5). Here is a man who is clearly "saved," to use modern evangelical terminology. He has not only been invited to the feast, he has accepted the call, and gotten inside. He is a "friend," a member of the inner circle, even closer than those people who called Jesus "Lord" and prophesied in His name and drove out demons and worked miracles, but of whom Jesus says, "I never knew you" (Matt. 7:23).

Yet he refused to wear the king's clothes. He didn't observe the proper protocol. And when the king asked him why, he had no excuse, for there was none. He couldn't plead that he hadn't enough money to buy such fine clothing, because the clothing was free. And so he was excluded from the feast— cast into outer darkness. What was so tragic is that this man had heard and accepted the gospel call. But the clothes weren't right. The robe was missing.

And evidently his case is not unique or uncommon, because the conclusion of the parable—the main point that Jesus wanted to make—is this: many are called, but few are chosen.

I can think of several other parables that reinforce that point. First, there is the miniparable in Matthew 7:13, 14:

> Enter through the narrow gate. For wide is the gate and broad is the road that leads to destruction, and many enter through it. But small is the gate and narrow the road that leads to life, and only a few find it.

This is another way of saying "Many are called, but few are chosen." Then there is the parable of the net:

> Once again, the kingdom of heaven is like a net that was let down into the lake and caught all kinds of fish. When it was full, the fishermen pulled it up on the shore. Then they sat down and collected the good fish in baskets, but threw the bad away (Matt. 13:47, 48).

Notice that in this parable most of the fish in the sea never get into the net in the first place. But even those fish *in the gospel net* face a final sort between the good and the bad. Even those who answer the gospel call are judged before they are chosen.

Then there is the parable of the vine:

> I am the true vine, and my Father is the gardener. He cuts off every branch in me that bears no fruit, while every branch that does bear fruit he prunes so that it will be even more fruitful. You are already clean because of the

word I have spoken to you. Remain in me, and I will remain in you. No branch can bear fruit by itself; it must remain in the vine. Neither can you bear fruit unless you remain in me. I am the vine; you are the branches. If a man remains in me and I in him, he will bear much fruit; apart from me you can do nothing. If anyone does not remain in me, he is like a branch that is thrown away and withers; such branches are picked up, thrown into the fire and burned (John 15:1-6).

Those that stay in the vine get pruned back so that they bear more fruit. Those who start out in the vine but allow themselves to get separated from the vine wither away, and are thrown into the fire. Once again Jesus tells a story in which the conclusion is that even the insiders, or former insiders, face a final judgment of some sort.

We can hardly ignore the clear teaching of these parables that all make essentially the same point. And of course the Scriptures are quite clear that the saints do face final judgment. "God will bring to judgment both the righteous and the wicked" (Eccl. 3:17). Jesus gave us another picture of the judgment in His parable of the sheep and the goats in Matthew 25:31-46, which involves everyone, good and evil. Paul told the Christians in Rome and Corinth, "We will all stand before God's judgment seat" (Rom. 14:10). "For we must all appear before the judgment seat of Christ, that each one may receive what is due him for the things done while in the body, whether good or bad" (2 Cor. 5:10). Hebrews 10:29, 30 says that those who have been sanctified by the blood of the covenant but who have treated that blood as an unholy thing will be rejected, and concludes, "The Lord will judge his people" (Heb. 10:30).

I believe it was in the early 1990s that I picked up an issue of *Loma Linda Scope*. Ten former Adventist physicians had been invited to write brief essays explaining why they were no longer Seventh-day Adventists. I was startled to discover that two of the 10 cited the same passage, John 5:24, as their rationale for leaving the church:

I tell you the truth, whoever hears my word and believes him who sent me has eternal life and will not be condemned; he has crossed over from death to life.

On the Internet one can find other testimonies that cite this same verse as reason for leaving the church. It seems rather important to look into this text, which has been responsible for creating so many ex-Adventists. What is so special about this passage? Why does it have this effect?

The Greek word translated "condemned" here in the NIV is *krisis,* which is sometimes translated "judgment." Our critics contend that this passage teaches that those who believe in Jesus will never have to face any sort of judgment. By choosing Jesus we pass out of the realm of eschatological jeopardy and into that of unconditional security.

Unfortunately, expertise in endocrinology does not necessarily correlate with expertise in exegesis. That is, medical doctors don't necessarily have a lot of expertise in interpretation of Scripture. To arrive at this conclusion one has to ignore all the passages that clearly teach a judgment for believers. But one also has to ignore the context of John 5:24. That little word *krisis* pops up again five verses later, where it clearly means "condemned," since it is the reward of the wicked:

A time is coming when all who are in their graves will hear his voice and come out—those who have done good will rise to live, and those who have done evil will rise to be condemned [krisis] (John 5:28, 29).

That is why the NIV translates "condemned" in 5:24. Clearly, *krisis* here is not a neutral judicial process but the negative outcome of that process. What the believer escapes is not the trial but the guilty verdict.

Equally important are the tenses of the verbs. Our critics interpret John 5:24 as if it said, "He who has believed [aorist tense] will not come [future tense] into condemnation." But there are no past tenses and no future tenses in the Greek of this verse. The verbs are all in the present tense. In other words the sense is: "He who is hearing My words and is believing on Him that sent Me is not coming into condemnation." As long as a person keeps on believing, he is not under *krisis.* It is impossible to get from this text the idea that once you have believed in the past, you will never be judged in the future.

The closest parallels to this passage are John 3:18, "Whoever believes in him is not condemned [krisis] but whoever does not believe stands condemned already;" and Romans 8:1, "There is therefore now no condemnation [krisis] for those who are in Christ Jesus." Romans 8 goes on to describe "those who are in Christ Jesus" as those "who do not live according to the sinful nature but according to the Spirit" (verse 4).

John does not teach that judgment for the believer is something wholly in the past, or is merely an existential event in which we judge ourselves by choosing or rejecting Christ. It is but a small step from that to the position that the Resurrection and Second Coming are also past or existential—a heresy condemned already in the New Testament (2 Tim. 2:18; 1 Cor. 15:12). John clearly teaches that a day of judgment is coming, but that we can have confidence in it: "Love is made complete among us so that *we will have confidence on the day of judgment,* because in this world we are like him" (1 John 4:17). Please notice that, according to John, we *can have confidence* in the day of judgment, and that this confidence is because "in this world *we are like him.*" That is good Johannine theology (more about this in a later chapter).

Nothing can ever snatch one of Jesus' sheep out of the hand of the Shepherd (John 10:29). But of course the sheep are defined as those who follow the Shepherd (verse 27). There is no security in unfaithfulness.

CHAPTER 5

The Robe
in the Old Testament

If you read every parable found in the Gospels, you will discover that more of them end on a note of threat than on a note of comfort. Jesus' message made people very uncomfortable. It shook people up. It challenged their complacency. In the previous chapter we reviewed some of the parables of Jesus that speak of a final judgment even for believers. We discussed the parable of the robe, and got to the point where one man was tied up and cast into outer darkness because he was not wearing the wedding garment. But we never discussed the meaning of the robe. Frankly, this robe is nowhere explicitly defined in the parable. We have to ask how Jesus' audience would have understood it.

In order to understand a Biblical metaphor, it is necessary to trace it back through Scripture. What exactly is the textual history of this metaphor? Let's start with Isaiah.

> I delight greatly in the Lord; my soul rejoices in my God. For he has clothed me with garments of salvation and arrayed me in a robe of righteousness, as a bridegroom adorns his head like a priest, and as a bride adorns herself with her jewels (Isa. 61:10).

The clothes in this passage obviously have something to do with righteousness. One thing is quite clear: the garment is given us by God. He clothes us with garments of salvation. All righteousness of any sort is His gift, just as in the parable of the wedding garment, where the robes are provided.

However, even this passage speaks of the priest *donning* headgear, and the bride *adorning herself* with jewels, and this is compared, not contrasted, with what God does for us. Another passage that uses the same metaphor of putting on clothing is Job 29:14-16:

> I put on righteousness as my clothing; justice was my robe and my turban. I was eyes to the blind and feet to the lame. I was a father to the needy; I took up the case of the stranger.

What was it that Job was putting on? It was righteous behavior, actual good deeds. "I was eyes to the blind and feet to the lame." There is nothing forensic or imputed about it. It is same robe as in Revelation 19:8, "fine linen stands for the righteous acts of the saints." What we are going to discover is that this metaphor is used consistently all the way through Scripture: the robe always has something to do with actual righteous behavior. In no case does it clearly refer to forensic, imputed, "as if" righteousness.

Even evil behavior is described in terms of clothing. Psalm 73:6 speaks of the wicked who "clothe themselves with violence." Psalm 109:18, 19 speaks of the wicked man who "wore cursing as his garment; it entered into his body like water, into his bones like oil. May it be like a cloak wrapped about him, like a belt tied forever around him." Clearly, the robe represents behavior, whether good or evil.

Other passages in Isaiah also use this metaphor. "He [God] put on righteousness as his breastplate, and the helmet of salvation on his head; he put on the garments of vengeance and wrapped himself in zeal as in a cloak" (Isa. 59:17). Isaiah 61:3 speaks of the "garment of praise" instead of the spirit of despair. Praise is something we do. So is vengeance.

One passage, Isaiah 64:6, is commonly misunderstood to suggest that human righteousness *at its best* is no better than "filthy rags." But Isaiah is not describing exemplary behavior at all. He is saying that his people have become backslidden, their actions are corrupt. He describes a people who never pray. Read the verse again, in context:

> All of us have become like one who is unclean, and all our righteous acts are like filthy rags; we all shrivel up like a leaf, and like the wind our sins sweep us away. No one calls on your name or strives to lay hold of you (Isa. 64:6, 7).

"Filthy rags" is a description of a nation in a backslidden state. Their spiritual "garments" have become polluted. Once again, the metaphor of a garment is descriptive of character.

Is this garment of righteousness a gift from God or not? Does He put it on us, or do we put it on? The Bible uses both metaphors. Even when we are given a new set of clothes, we still have to put it on. When we plant broccoli, do we actually grow the broccoli? Not really. We may help it along with water and fertilizer, but the growth is a mystery of God.

But without us working in the garden there would be no broccoli for dinner.

You have no doubt heard the story of the traveler who was walking in the countryside one day and he came across a farmer who was standing by his fence admiring his fields. As he watched the corn waving in the breeze, the traveler walked over and stood by the farmer in silence, following his gaze. Feeling especially pious that day, perhaps, the stranger said, "Isn't it beautiful what God has done here?" The farmer quietly replied, "Well, you should have seen what this field looked like when God had it to Himself!"

I used to wonder why Ezekiel urged his people to "rid yourselves of all the offenses you have committed, and *get a new heart and a new spirit*" (Eze. 18:30, 31). Ezekiel knew, of course, that the new heart is something only God can give:

> I will sprinkle clean water on you, and you will be clean; I will cleanse you from all your impurities and from all your idols. I will give you a new heart and put a new spirit in you; I will remove from you your heart of stone and give you a heart of flesh. And I will put my Spirit in you and move you to follow my decrees and be careful to keep my laws (Eze. 36:25-27).

We can never create a new heart for ourselves because we can only wash ourselves on the outside. We cannot wash our hearts. That is something only God can do. And it is something that can be done only with blood. But we have a part to play in the process.

When Adam and Eve tried to make fig leaves for themselves, I imagine that God, after He showed up on the scene and talked with them, must have shaken His head sadly, then called over their pet lamb. Then—horror of horrors—God took the innocent creature and slit its throat and spilled its blood on the ground. Adam and Eve must have been in shock, perhaps retching with nausea, having never seen death before. What have we *done?* The price is too high!

"Oh no," I hear God say, "the price is much higher than this!"

But the death of that lamb enabled God to replace their inadequate coverings with a garment that would keep them a lot warmer than fig leaves when the first cold winds began to blow in Eden.

Of course, Adam and Eve had a part to play. They had to put on the skins, and keep wearing them.

Let's look at the symbol of the robe as used in Zechariah. There we see Joshua, who as the high priest represents all of Israel, standing in filthy clothing, blackened by fire. But God has an amazing transformation in mind for him: a completely new wardrobe. If God can create a sun, He can recreate a son. "Joshua was dressed in filthy clothes as he stood before the angel. The angel said to those who were standing before him, 'Take off his filthy clothes.' Then he said to Joshua, 'See, I have taken away your sin, and I will put rich garments on you'" (Zech. 3:3, 4). Compare this with Psalm 132:9, 16, which speaks of the priests being clothed with righteousness and with salvation.

Notice that the new clothes in Zechariah 3 are not put on over the old. The old, filthy rags are taken off. The concept of our filthy rags being covered by Christ's righteousness may have some homiletical validity, but it is not a Biblical metaphor. Nowhere does the Bible speak of a clean garment being placed over a filthy one to hide it. Revelation 3:18 does speak of clothing our nakedness (cf. 16:15), but this is quite different from the idea of wearing two different robes, one dirty, one clean. That is contrary to both common sense and Scripture. The dirty robe comes off when the clean one goes on. Nowhere in Scripture does the robe ever represent a forensic camouflage which hides the filthy reality beneath.

Even in the parable of the prodigal son the father tells the servants, "Quick! Bring the best robe and put it on him. Put a ring on his finger and sandals on his feet. Bring the fattened calf and kill it" (Luke 15:22, 23). These things would require a bit of time. The servants would have given the son a bath before dressing him up for the feast. I don't know anyone who puts clean clothes on over dirty ones. The problem with such a metaphor is the implication that Christ's righteousness becomes a cloak for continued impurity.

> No repentance is genuine that does not work reformation. The righteousness of Christ is not a cloak to cover unconfessed and unforsaken sin; it is a principle of life that transforms the character and controls the conduct (*The Desire of Ages*, pp. 555, 556).

Joshua in Zechariah 3 stands as the representative of his people. The sin of the people was imputed to the priest as their representative, and vice versa: the sin of the priest was imputed to the people (Lev. 4:3). The people were "in" the priest, and what happens to the priest happens to the people. Here God deals with the entire nation in the person of their representative, Joshua, which is the Hebrew version of the name Jesus.

The cleansing of Joshua is only the beginning of the story. Now there is something that Joshua has to do to retain his new status, as we read the rest of the passage:

> The angel of the Lord gave this charge to Joshua: "This is what the Lord Almighty says: 'If you will walk in my ways and keep my requirements, then you will govern my house and have charge of my courts, and I will give you a place among these standing here'" (Zech. 3:6, 7).

God offered Joshua a place "among these standing here," i.e., among those assistants of the angel of the Lord, who were no doubt angels themselves. The garments of salvation were a free gift to Joshua. Zechariah could not earn them. But the condition is that Joshua must "walk in my ways and keep my requirements."

The concept of something that is free yet conditional is not really a paradox; it is not even difficult to understand, because many things in life are like this. In America "life, liberty, and the pursuit of happiness" are considered an "unalienable right" with which we have been endowed by our Creator. Yet we may lose our liberty and be confined to prison if we break the law.

Captain Chesley Sullenberger seems to have an uncanny ability to land large aircraft on water that was not made for amphibious landings. Suppose that he were to offer you a free ticket on an invitation-only flight from New York to Los Angeles, California. That would be a high honor! You did nothing to earn the flight; you did not pay one penny toward the ticket. All you have to do is receive it. It is gratis.

But even after you hold the ticket in your sweaty palms—in fact, even after you are seated on the plane—there are still conditions. If you try to smuggle a weapon on board, your ticket will definitely not be honored. If you were to harass the flight attendant, you might never make it to Los Angeles. Your trip may be aborted by an unpleasant stop in Denver.

The flight is free but conditional. You can get yourself thrown off the plane. But as long as you stay on the plane, you are destined for Los Angeles. In fact you are *predestined* for Los Angeles, since that's what your ticket said from the moment you got it, long before you boarded the flight.

Salvation is like that. God's grace is free yet conditional. And, yes, we are predestined for heaven. As long as we stay aboard the gospel train.

Most people are familiar with Hans Christian Anderson's parable of the emperor's new clothes. It has been translated into over 100 languages. The story goes like this: an emperor who cares for nothing but his wardrobe hires two weavers who promise him the finest suit of clothes. Their fabric, they claim, is invisible to anyone who is unfit for his position or "just hopelessly stupid." The emperor himself cannot see the cloth, but pretends that he can for fear of appearing unfit. His ministers do the same. When the swindlers report that the suit is finished, they dress him in mime and the emperor then marches in procession before his subjects.

His politically correct subjects, not wanting to be rude, compliment the emperor on his new vestment. Finally a child in the crowd yells out the ghastly truth that the emperor is wearing nothing at all. Others take up the cry. The emperor cringes, suspecting the assertion is true, but holds himself up proudly and continues the procession.

There is a ditch on either side of the highway of grace. One is legalism, another is antinomianism. Both ditches are full of old shipwrecks of faith, but the left ditch—the libertine ditch—is much better populated, since asceticism is not exactly popular, but loose living is. The number of lives being destroyed today by unrestrained indulgence in sex, drugs, and alcohol is at all-time epidemic levels. We live in an age that downplays the need for purity of life. Today it is those who stress the need for holy living that are swimming upstream. Here, then, is an imaginary conversation which I call the parable of the emperor's *new* new clothes.

"What are you doing?"

"Friend, today I'm resting in the grace of God."

"No, I mean just now. Why are you watching that kind of trash?"

"Are you judging me? Perhaps you don't understand the gospel. My only righteousness is the imputed righteousness of Jesus Christ! In it there is not a thread of human devising. I have nothing to contribute to my salvation at all. The gospel is plus nothing and minus nothing. There is nothing for me to do. When I sin, I have no worries, because Jesus is my righteousness, and God does not look at my life, but at His life. I will never be judged based on my behavior, but on His. I am forever secure in the arms of Jesus. He will never turn His back on one of His own."

"But . . . what you just did is unethical and dishonest, something you would be ashamed of if published on the front page of the newspaper. Don't you think you should confess that?"

"That's between God and me. My righteousness is not based on anything I can do, not even confession of sin. It is based upon His doing and dying. Those who believe in Jesus do not come into judgment. Don't worry, I'll take care of it. Besides, you have no right to judge another believer who is fully clothed in His righteousness."

"But . . . but . . . my friend, spiritually speaking, *You're naked!*"

Every believer has an invitation to eat at the King's table. And along with the invitation, the King has provided us with everything we need, including a new set of clothes so that we will be fit for the divine dining hall. Our part is simple: wear the clothes. "Behold, I come like a thief! Blessed is he who stays awake and keeps his clothes with him, so that he may not go naked and be shamefully exposed" (Rev. 16:15).

CHAPTER 6

The Robe
in the New Testament

In the previous chapter we argued that the robe of righteousness, nowhere defined in the parable Jesus told in Matthew 22, represents what it does everywhere else in Scripture: it represents righteousness. Not imputed, forensic, or "as if" righteousness, but actual character. But so far we have looked only at those passages in the Old Testament that use this metaphor. Now let's cross over into the New Testament.

Paul uses the metaphor of the robe in Colossians. And it still represents behavior:

> You must rid yourselves of all such things as these: anger, rage, malice, slander, and filthy language from your lips. Do not lie to each other, since you have taken off your old self with its practices and have put on the new self, which is being renewed in knowledge in the image of its Creator. . . . Therefore, as God's chosen people, holy and dearly loved, clothe yourselves with compassion, kindness, humility, gentleness and patience (Col. 3:8-12).

The old self here is our old habits, old sins. Notice that it can be taken off and put on. Notice also that the new is not put on over the old. Off with the old, on with the new—that is the scriptural metaphor. The Holy Spirit empowers us to take off the old deeds of the flesh and put on the new fruits of the Spirit. But the taking off and putting on is an act of the will.

When I feel like saying something I might regret later, it is an act of the will to take off the old self with its anger, rage, and malice, and put on the new self with its kindness. Every Christian makes a dozen such decisions a day. Without God we couldn't do it; without us God won't do it.

The picture becomes clearer when we compare two other passages that use the clothing metaphor:

All of you who were baptized into Christ have clothed yourselves with Christ (Gal. 3:27).

Clothe yourselves with the Lord Jesus Christ, and do not think about how to gratify the desires of the sinful nature (Rom. 13:14).

Here is a fascinating paradox: we have already clothed ourselves with Christ. That happened when we were baptized. Why, then, does Paul tell us to do it again? Isn't once enough? Can't we trust our salvation? And what does putting on Christ mean? In context Paul's meaning is obvious: he is talking about holy living.

> The night is nearly over; the day is almost here. So let us put aside the deeds of darkness and put on the armor of light. Let us behave decently, as in the daytime, not in orgies and drunkenness, not in sexual immorality and debauchery, not in dissension and jealousy. Rather, clothe yourselves with the Lord Jesus Christ, and do not think about how to gratify the desires of the sinful nature (Rom. 13:12-14).

Putting on Jesus is something that must be done every day. Paul's message here is: Become what you are. Live up to your title. We must reaffirm our status daily to maintain our status. There is no such thing as once saved, always saved any more than there is once lost, always lost. It is not that we fall in and out of salvation with each sin we commit. That's silly. Do you abandon your pet dog to the animal shelter every time he messes on the carpet, or your cat every time she claws the drapes? God understands that we will sometimes fail in our fight with the demands of the sinful nature. But if we get up whenever we fall, we will grow strong in the fight.

When I was in college there were two different Greek teachers in the religion department. Several theology students were sitting around talking one day trying to decide which class to take. We compared and contrasted, and finally agreed on this: With one professor, you start out the class with an A, and then struggle all semester to keep it. With the other, you start with an F and struggle to work your way to an A.

Salvation works a little like the first professor's class. We start with an A, and struggle to keep up with the Holy Spirit as He leads us to ever greater heights of spiritual maturity. The Spirit will not let us rest long on our laurels, lest we become flabby Christians. If we are coasting, we're not growing.

The man who came into the wedding supper without the wedding garment was called, but not chosen. He may have clothed himself with Christ, but he didn't keep keeping on. He was still wearing the old man. The old lifestyle.

I'm glad we've more or less gotten past the debates in the church in the 1970s and 1980s over justification versus. sanctification. It is foolish to argue about which is more important, because God justifies no one whom He does not sanctify and vice versa. Remember the words of the old hymn: "Be of sin the *double* cure, save from wrath, and make me pure." Another old hymn goes: "What can wash away my sin? Nothing but the blood of Jesus. What can make me pure within? Nothing but the blood. . . . "

You can't have one without the other.

The Holy Spirit through Peter gives us a solemn warning about the consequences of getting our robe dirty by wallowing in the mud:

> If they have escaped the corruption of the world by knowing our Lord and Savior Jesus Christ and are again entangled in it and overcome, they are worse off at the end than they were at the beginning. It would have been better for them not to have known the way of righteousness, than to have known it and then to turn their backs on the sacred command that was passed on to them. Of them the proverbs are true: "A dog returns to its vomit," and, "A sow that is washed goes back to her wallowing in the mud" (2 Peter 2:20-22).

A lawyer can be disbarred. A president can be impeached. A minister defrocked. And a child of God can have their name blotted out of the book of life if they turn their back on God (Rev. 3:5).

Peter is another writer who uses the metaphor of the robe. "Clothe yourselves with humility," he writes (1 Peter 5:5). Again, the robe represents behavior.

The book of Revelation has a lot to say about the robe. First of all we start with a passage that defines the robe exactly:

> Let us rejoice and be glad and give him glory! For the wedding of the Lamb has come, and his bride has made herself ready. Fine linen, bright and clean, was given her to wear. (Fine linen stands for the righteous acts of the saints) (Rev. 19:7-8).

This passage comes as a bit of a shock to some evangelicals who define righteousness in strictly forensic terms. One of my less traditional church members years ago startled me after discovering this verse by saying, "Well, maybe John just didn't understand the gospel!"

Here is the most explicit definition of the robe of righteousness in Scripture: it is the "righteous acts" or "righteous deeds" (depending on translation) of the saints. This meaning of the metaphor is consistent from Genesis to Revelation. And the bride in this text—the church—*makes herself* ready. Yet the bridal dress is a gift of God, woven in the loom of heaven. It is not something we create, or buy, or purchase, or weave, or sew, or work up, or achieve. It is only available from heaven's department store, on God's credit card.

But we have to put it on. And even after that it can get dirty! And what happens then?

> "Blessed are those who wash their robes, that they may have the right to the tree of life and may go through the gates into the city (Rev. 22:14).

When Israel was gathered around Mount Sinai in preparation for the giving of the law, God told them to wash their clothes (Ex. 19:10, 14). To come into the presence of God, clean garments are essential.

What is this garment that can be soiled (Rev. 3:4) and must be washed (Rev. 7:14; 22:14)? Clearly it cannot represent Christ's imputed righteousness, because that robe is always perfect, cannot be soiled, and never needs washing. The robe here, as everywhere else in Scripture, represents character. It is the same robe as the "righteous deeds" of Rev. 19:8.

> When we submit ourselves to Christ, the heart is united with His heart, the will is merged in His will, the mind becomes one with His mind, the thoughts are brought into captivity to Him; we live His life. This is what it means to be clothed with the garment of His righteousness (*Christ's Object Lessons,* p. 312).

Ellen White is reflecting perfectly good Johannine theology here.

But how does this theology fit with the Pauline idea of imputed righteousness? In Paul's classical chapter on righteousness by faith, Romans 4, he uses repeatedly the term *elogisthe,* which means "imputed" or "credited" or "reckoned" or "calculated," a metaphor taken from the accounting profession. When we believe, Christ's righteousness is placed to our account from the start. This happens by faith, says Paul, entirely apart from works.

But John does not speak of salvation in quite the same way. He uses a different metaphor, one every mother can understand.

Mothers are always looking for the perfect detergent; one that will take out any stain. Something that produces whiter whites and brighter brights after a wash. Several laundry detergents claim to grant this wish. Before dishwashers became common we used to see lots of commercials touting dishwashing detergents that cut through the grease but were gentle on the hands. The world has detergents for everything.

But no detergent ever produced on earth can remove a stain on the inside. Only the blood of Jesus can do that.

My wife Carol and I have a wonderful little cavalier "King Charles" spaniel that we love, and a cat too, but, well . . . spot remover is a wonderful thing.

People who approach the subject of righteousness from a Pauline perspective sometimes assert that everything we do is defiled by sin. On that point they are surely correct. Here is a simple way to understand this.

God has the same problem with us that we do with our pets. *They defile our sanctuary!* They shed, making us a walking powder puff of alien hair. Just jumping up into our lap is an act of defilement. It gets worse. Even when they use the litter box, like they're supposed to, it is offensive to our olfactory apparatus—not to mention the worst-case scenario when they start "thinking outside the box." Sometimes they jump up on the kitchen table or favorite sofa that we have declared out of bounds to them—our "holy things," from their standpoint. Their presence is defiling.

Still, we don't throw them out (although repeated urinating on the furniture might do it) because we love them. We don't mind the medical expense and the dirt and the inconvenience because we love the excited wag of the tail, the purring in the lap—the animal version of worship. We love how they love us. And after all, we chose them and paid the price for them, knowing in advance the problems they would bring.

Our pets are a parable of our relationship to God. God craves our fellowship and our worship. Our praise blesses Him like a cat's purr blesses us. Unfortunately, our very presence is defiling. But God packs some potent heavenly stain removers.

Hebrews 9:14 promises that "the blood of Christ" will "cleanse our consciences from acts that lead to death, so that we may serve the living God!" So "let us draw near to God with a sincere heart in full assurance of faith, having our hearts sprinkled to cleanse us from a guilty conscience and having our bodies washed with pure water" (Heb. 10:22). Jesus' blood is the ultimate detergent. The redeemed are defined as those who have washed their robes of character.

> These are they who have come out of the great tribulation; they have washed their robes and made them white in the blood of the Lamb (Rev. 7:14).

It is the blood of Jesus Christ, God's Son, that cleanses us from all sin. It is only through the blood of Christ, not through mere human effort, that our robe of character can be washed and cleansed.

> There is a fountain filled with blood,
> Drawn from Immanuel's veins;

And sinners plunged beneath that flood,
Lose all their guilty stains.

Obviously this is not just a one-time thing that happens on the day of our baptism. Every day we come to God in prayer anew and say, "Father, I give You my life today. Teach me to follow You. Wash me and make me white, and let me walk in the light of Your countenance."

But if we walk in the light, as he is in the light, we have fellowship with one another, and the blood of Jesus, his Son, purifies us from all sin (1 John 1:7).

In the 1953 film *The Robe* Roman tribune Marcellus Gallio is a cynical and hardened man. He insults the Roman Emperor Caligula and so gets sent off to Jerusalem. There he finds himself in charge of the crucifixion of Jesus. During the crucifixion Gallio wins Jesus' robe in a game of dice. But he is haunted by it, and comes to believe that it is bewitched.

The robe is acquired by Demetrius, a Christian, an escaped slave of Marcellus. Marcellus sets out to find Demetrius in order to destroy the robe and the curse. When he finds him, he begins to question his spiritually bankrupt life, and Rome's cruelty. Ultimately, Marcellus finds faith, and becomes a Christian and a martyr.

Marcellus went to a great deal of expense to find the robe. But you and I can have that priceless, seamless robe today just for the asking, because when Christ wore the scarlet robe of sin for us, He then took off His white robe of righteousness and gave it to us. If you haven't already done it, go down to the fountain and wash your clothes. Take that priceless, spotless robe today, and put it on, and keep it on, because the feast is almost ready.

CHAPTER 7

Assurance?

The white-haired patriarch lay on his bed, his breathing uneven now. Death crouched just beyond the door, in the darkness outside the circle of flickering lamplight. Forming a boundary against the darkness were 12 strong sons who gathered close around their father to catch his dying blessing. The story begins in Genesis 49:1: "Then Jacob called for his sons and said: 'Gather around so I can tell you what will happen to you in days to come.'"

Sometimes it seems that individuals are given the gift of prophecy on their deathbed. Let's look at Jacob's deathbed prophecy for his sons and then study how it shaped the fortunes of his descendants.

Jacob had 12 sons, but let's focus on just two: the tribe of Levi, and the tribe of Judah. First Levi. According to Jacob's prediction, things didn't look good for Levi:

> Simeon and Levi are brothers—their swords are weapons of violence. Let me not enter their council, let me not join their assembly, for they have killed men in their anger and hamstrung oxen as they pleased. Cursed be their anger, so fierce, and their fury, so cruel! I will scatter them in Jacob and disperse them in Israel (Gen. 49:5-7).

Bad news for Levi. How would you feel if you were Levi or one of his sons with a curse like that hanging over you? What sort of a future would you envision for your descendants? Pretty discouraging, huh! We need to look at the reason for this curse. It flowed from Levi's sin of violence.

The story is told in Genesis 34. Shechem, the son of a pagan king, had violated Levi's sister Dinah. Now Shechem was not a bad man. He wanted to do the right thing and marry her. So he came to her brothers and said, "I'll pay you whatever you want, but I love your sister. Name your bride price."

So what did Levi do? He lied to Shechem and his clan, played a trick on them, then attacked them by surprise and slew every male in the whole city. Levi's violent anger twisted his future for a long time. A crime of passion can twist a destiny in the wrong direction for many years, and sometimes for many generations.

Jacob predicted that Levi would reap what he had sown as a man of violence. But what about Judah? What does the prophecy say about his fortunes? Things are really looking good for Judah:

> Judah, your brothers will praise you; your hand will be on the neck of your enemies; your father's sons will bow down to you. You are a lion's cub, O Judah; you return from the prey, my son. Like a lion he crouches and lies down, like a lioness—who dares to rouse him? The scepter will not depart from Judah, nor the ruler's staff from between his feet, until he comes to whom it belongs and the obedience of the nations is his. He will tether his donkey to a vine, his colt to the choicest branch; he will wash his garments in wine, his robes in the blood of grapes. His eyes will be darker than wine, his teeth whiter than milk (Gen. 49:8-12).

What a wonderful blessing for Judah! His tribe will rule in Israel. From him will come the Messiah, the conqueror who will conquer the nations and bring Israel to greatness. If you were a son of Judah, would you not have high hopes being born under such a powerful birthright promise as that? Would you not have assurance that you were the chosen tribe, the crème de la crème, the remnant of the remnant?

Assurance is a wonderful thing, isn't it!

Well, Jacob died, and time passed. The tribes multiplied and left Egypt in the Exodus under Moses. They wandered in the wilderness for a generation, until eventually Moses himself died. Just before he took that last long walk up the mountain, he too bestowed a prophetic blessing on each of the 12 tribes, as was traditional at the death of the leader of a clan in ancient times. Now remember: Jacob's deathbed prophecy blessed Judah and cursed Levi. So let's see what Moses had to say about the future of Levi and Judah.

> And this he said about Judah: "Hear, O Lord, the cry of Judah; bring him to his people. With his own hands he defends his cause. Oh, be his help against his foes!" (Deut. 33:7).

Well, it's something, but it's a lot less than the ringing praise of Jacob's prophecy. It's much shorter. Judah's star has fallen a bit. But now, what has happened to Levi? Let's see:

> About Levi he said: "Your Thummim and Urim belong to the man you favored. You tested him at Massah; you contended with him at the waters of Meribah. He said of his father and mother, 'I have no regard for them.' He did not recognize his brothers or acknowledge his own children, but he watched over your word and guarded your covenant. He teaches your precepts to Jacob and your law to Israel. He offers incense before you and whole burnt offerings on your altar. Bless all his skills, O Lord, and be pleased with the work of his hands. Smite the loins of those who rise up against him; strike his foes till they rise no more" (Deut. 33:8-11).

Amazing. Levi has been promoted! Do you see the difference? In the earlier prophecy of Jacob (Gen. 49:5-12) Judah receives the biggest blessing of all of the 12 brothers, and Levi is cursed. But in the later prophecy of Moses (Deut. 33:7-11) Judah is passed over and Levi receives the biggest blessing.

What happened?

The destiny of the tribes had been changed by their intervening behavior. A crisis point in Israel's history had changed the fortunes of Levi. Just after the incident of the molten calf, where Israel fell into idolatry at Sinai, Moses came down from the mountain full of righteous indignation, and demanded that his people take a stand against sin.

Remember, this is the self-sacrificing paragon of mercy that offered his life to God in exchange for his people.

Moses said, "Whoever is for the Lord, come to me." And all the Levites rallied to him. Then Moses told the Levites to take their swords and kill their brothers and friends and neighbors. They did. Three thousand people died.

Then Moses said, "You have been set apart to the Lord today, for you were against your own sons and brothers, and he has blessed you this day" (Ex. 32:26-29).

So was Moses more godlike when he interceded for his people, or when he slew the rebels? Think it over.

The Levites had distinguished themselves at Sinai by standing up for the Lord even though they had to turn against their own relatives to do so. In so doing they changed their hereditary curse into a blessing.

By the way, loyalty to God even at the cost of our blood relationships is still a requirement of those who would follow God. Jesus said, "For I have come to turn 'a man against his father, a daughter against her mother, a daughter-in-law against her mother-in-law—a man's enemies will be the members of his own household.' Anyone who loves his father or mother more than me is not worthy of me; anyone who loves his son or daughter more than me is not worthy of me" (Matt. 10:35-37). This does not of course involve violence; the authority to punish lies with the state (Rom. 13:4).

But back to Levi and Judah. The point of this story is that prophecy is not necessarily destiny. Things change. The black sheep can become the golden boy—and vice versa. Even the sort of assurance that comes from an inspired prophecy is only temporary.

Arnold J. Toynbee undertook as his life's work to answer the question "What makes great societies come into being and die? Under what conditions do civilizations thrive?" The results of his study are found in his multivolume work *A Study of History*. Here in a few paragraphs are the amazing conclusions that took him a lifetime of study to discover:

First of all, he rejects the hypothesis that there is an innately superior race.

Secondly, he also rejects the hypothesis that environments that produce easy and comfortable conditions are conducive to the development of great societies. On the contrary, he found that easy living does not make a society great. In fact, it hinders greatness. Balmy climates, for example, do not produce great civilizations.

Instead, Toynbee discovered that great societies arise as a response to the challenge of some great difficulty that spurs them on to unprecedented effort. The obstacle may be geographical, political, or military. It may even be a harsh climate. But as long as there is a challenge, something to fight against and overcome; as long as there are new frontiers, there is growth and vitality.

However, once a society achieves success, it often lowers its standards and becomes lax. Resting on its laurels, it becomes complacent and lazy, and decline sets in.

What do Toynbee's insights tell us about America? Well, America has had great challenges to meet. Just to take the more recent ones: For two generations after Hitler, it was the cold war with Russia. That was our defining struggle. Then we won that war, and life was easy for a decade. But easy street is a very dangerous place.

Today our defining struggle is with terrorism. That may be a blessing. For now it is our new frontier. It is one thing that keeps us on our toes.

Toynbee's principle also applies to churches. And the same principle applies to families and individuals. Riches and complacency produce decadence.

Arnold Toynbee tells us that great civilizations, and perhaps also great churches, and even great Christians, need a challenge, an untamed frontier, a thorn in the flesh, a disadvantage, an uncertainty, to grow. God could remove all our uncertainties in a moment by drawing aside the veil and showing us the end from the beginning. But revealing the future is the most demotivating thing I can think of. In fact, as a rule, *the removal of risk brings decadence and eventually destroys the system.*

This is why socialism (state-enforced communism, as opposed to voluntary communalism) doesn't work. Imagine what would happen to an academy or college class who were told that everyone would receive the same grade on their next assignment—an average of the grades of all the papers. Suppose this were repeated over time. What would happen to the class average? Would it go up or down? Would the students study harder and harder? Almost certainly not. The class average would decline, and the class would be demotivated. When we reward failure and penalize success, we get more failure and less success. Jesus' rule is pretty much the opposite: "I tell you that to everyone who has, more will be given, but as for the one who has nothing, even what he has will be taken away" (Luke 19:26).

Revealing individual futures is a removal of risk. If we knew the future we would cease to strive. If we knew we would ultimately be lost, we would give up in despair and not even try to live for God. If we knew we would ultimately be saved, most of us would rest on our laurels and not work so hard for the kingdom. That is just human nature. God wisely refuses to give us that ultimate certainty, because He does not want us ever to become completely comfortable on the journey lest we settle down and cease to make progress. We walk by faith, not by sight.

Too much security takes the edge off. A little insecurity keeps us fresh. At least that's how it works for codfish.

At the turn of the century codfish were much in demand on the East Coast. News of this tasty fish eventually spread across the country to the West Coast. But it took a while to figure out how to ship the fish across the country and still keep it fresh. At first they tried shipping the frozen fish by rail, the fastest means at the time. But the resulting product, when cooked, was mushy and lacked flavor. Next someone had the bright idea of shipping the fish in railroad cars turned into huge saltwater aquariums. The fish arrived alive, but when prepared they were still mushy and tasteless.

Someone analyzed the problem and discovered that the natural enemy of codfish was the catfish. So they began to put a few catfish in the codfish tanks. Those catfish chased the codfish all the way across the country to the West Coast. Now when they were prepared the fish were deliciously flaky, with the same flavor as when caught fresh and prepared on the East Coast. The catfish kept the cod from becoming stale. They made them fresh.

There is no such thing as unconditional assurance—even for a church. If you disagree with this, then please read carefully what must be the most unconditional-sounding promises God ever made in Jeremiah 31:35-37. No matter what, God says, Israel will never cease to be a nation. I will never reject them. How could Israel ever lose its status as God's promised people with promises like that?

If Seventh-day Adventists believe they are unconditionally elected as a denomination, that is very bad news for the church. We will grow ever more complacent and lose our edge entirely. Because the principles that apply to nations also apply to churches, societies, schools, and individuals.

There is an old saying that the job of the pastor is to comfort the afflicted and afflict the comfortable. Maintaining the balance is not easy. A good pastor must be gospel- and grace-oriented, because everyone is fighting a hard battle, and most people need encouragement more than judgment. At the same time a good pastor, like a good coach, will motivate his members to a higher level of purity, spiritual maturity, and activity in sharing. On rare occasions public rebuke is even called for (1 Tim. 5:20).

There are two kinds of churches in the world: those whose goal is to make people feel good, and those whose goal is to make good people.

False religion says, "It doesn't matter how you live; you're okay in Jesus." True religion says, "If you think you are standing firm, be careful that you don't fall!" (1 Cor. 10:12).

False religion says, "You need to feel secure." True religion says, "Make your calling and election sure" (2 Peter 1:10).

We cannot take our salvation for granted any more than we can take our marriage for granted and expect it to last without effort on our part. In other words, we can't put our salvation on automatic pilot. We have to follow Jesus wherever He leads.

So one problem with assurance is psychological. Human nature being what it is, assurance very often leads to complacency. Comfort is not God's primary goal for us. C. S. Lewis once said, "If you want a religion to make you feel really comfortable, I certainly don't recommend Christianity" (*God in the Dock,* chapter "Answers to Questions on Christianity").

A subjective feeling of assurance can even have the deadly result of self-deception.

> Many will say to me on that day, "Lord, Lord, did we not prophesy in your name, and in your name drive out demons and perform many miracles?" Then I will tell them plainly, "I never knew you. Away from me, you evil-doers!" (Matt. 7:22, 23).

These people had assurance, but they didn't have Jesus. It is deadly to have a false assurance; to think you're climbing a mountain when you're actually about to walk over a cliff. That's much worse than the opposite problem. It's much better to be saved and think you're lost, than to be lost and think you're saved. Wouldn't you agree?

I would rather have a false fear than a false assurance. Wouldn't you? Of course, it's best not to have either. But if you're driving down the highway, which do you need most: a feeling of assurance about your tires—or a good set of tires?

So objective assurance is what we want, not subjective assurance. We need the reality, not just the feeling. Too much subjective assurance can actually be detrimental, because it's the person who is overconfident about his tires that is most likely to end up in the ditch because he neglects to examine them.

Self-examination is as good in the Christian life as it is for an automobile on the highway. That's why Paul says in 2 Corinthians 13:5, "Examine yourselves to see whether you are in the faith; test yourselves. Do you not realize that Christ Jesus is in you—unless, of course, you fail the test?" Jesus' own brother chimes in: "Blessed is the man who perseveres under trial, because when he has stood the test, he will receive the crown of life that God has promised to those who love him" (James 1:12). Peter adds: "Make your calling and election sure. For if you do these things, you will never fall" (2 Peter 1:10). And Paul says, "We want each of you to show this same diligence to the very end, in order to make your hope sure" (Heb. 6:11).

That subjective feeling of relaxed security that we call assurance can be a blessing, but it's not the holy grail. Like happiness, assurance is not a goal in itself, but a by-product of a certain way of life. When we understand what Jesus has done for us, and when we surrender to Him and see the Holy Spirit working in our lives, then we will be able to sing, with a new depth of meaning, "Blessed assurance, Jesus is mine."

CHAPTER 8

Taking God for Granted

Here is a chicken-and-egg problem for you. Which comes first: achievement or self-esteem? Do we achieve because we feel good about ourselves, or do we feel good about ourselves because we achieve?

This was a major controversy among educators for at least 20 years. The traditional position was that children who perform well in class will consequently feel good about themselves. But then more recent educational theories reversed this logic. They said that students must secure high self-esteem before they can hope to achieve. In other words, they must feel good about themselves before they can perform well in class.

Well, the research finally began to point in one direction a few years ago, and it tends to support the traditional position: achievement precedes self-esteem. High self-esteem does not produce excellence, and low self-esteem does not produce criminal behavior. In fact, researchers have found almost no correlation between low self-esteem and any number of social pathologies, including poor school performance, drug abuse, and teenage pregnancy.

A few years ago psychologists Harold W. Stevenson and James W. Stigler tested the academic skills of elementary school students in Japan, Taiwan, China, and the United States. In these tests the Asian students easily outperformed the Americans. But when the same students were asked how they felt about their subject skills, the Americans thought their academic prowess was much higher than the other students. In other words, those with the worst performance had the highest self-esteem. You can find their work in their book *The Learning Gap* (New York: Simon and Schuster, 1992). Since then much work has been done that shows that higher self-esteem does not lead to better performance. Today the self-esteem movement is essentially dead.

People with tenure tend to become arrogant, while the humble people do all the work, and make better employees. People who have tenure talk about protecting their rights instead of the privilege of duty. One study has even shown that inflated self-esteem among adolescent males can encourage violent behavior, so evidently it's possible to have too much self-esteem.

Perhaps that's why Jesus pronounced a blessing on the poor in spirit. It's possible to have too much assurance. This calls into question the benefits of feel-good religion.

Now assurance is certainly better than self-esteem. Our title to heaven is based on His life and not ours. Self-esteem focuses on self, while assurance focuses on something outside of self. We have assurance because we know that His grace is always greater than our sin. And we are promised that if we confess our sin, He is faithful and just to forgive us our sin, and cleanse us from all unrighteousness (1 John 1:9). That is quite possibly the greatest promise in the Bible.

However, we cannot take our relationship with God for granted any more than we can take our marriage for granted and expect it to last without any effort on our part.

Christians who are looking for unconditional assurance are looking for something even Paul didn't have. At least not when he wrote Philippians. Notice the strength of Paul's dedication to Jesus Christ:

> I consider everything a loss compared to the surpassing greatness of knowing Christ Jesus my Lord, for whose sake I have lost all things. I consider them rubbish, that I may gain Christ and be found in him, not having a right-eousness of my own that comes from the law, but that which is through faith in Christ—the righteousness that comes from God and is by faith.

Clearly, Paul is trusting in a righteousness that is outside of him, and not his own righteousness. He has all of that, but he is not resting on his laurels:

> I want to know Christ and the power of his resurrection and the fellowship of sharing in his sufferings, becoming like him in his death, and so, somehow,

to attain to the resurrection from the dead. Not that I have already obtained all this, or have already been made perfect, but I press on to take hold of that for which Christ Jesus took hold of me. Brothers, I do not consider myself yet to have taken hold of it.

What? Paul, the dedicated, self-sacrificing, self-disciplined apostle that gave his all to the gospel has not yet been granted spiritual tenure? He doesn't consider himself to have taken hold of eternal life yet? That's what he says. So what will he do?

But one thing I do: Forgetting what is behind and straining toward what is ahead, I press on toward the goal to win the prize for which God has called me heavenward in Christ Jesus. All of us who are mature should take such a view of things. (Phil. 3:8-15).

Paul says "I'm still working on it. I'm not there yet. I want to attain to the resurrection from the dead. I'm fighting a won battle, but I'm still fighting, see? And if you are a mature Christian, you should feel the same way." Even the great apostle Paul lived with uncertainty. Even he would not say, at this point in his life, "I am saved!"

What he *did* say is this: "This one thing I do." One thing.

In the motion picture *City Slickers* three middle-aged men join a cattle drive in their search for a sense of self. They learn the ropes from Curly, the seasoned and grizzled trail boss. After Mitch helps Curly deliver a calf, the two men have a serious conversation on the meaning of life. Curly holds up a single, gloved finger. "The meaning of life," the ancient cowboy explains, "is one thing. Just one thing."

"What? What's the one thing?" says Mitch.

"That's what you have to find out," says Curly.

Then Curly suddenly dies, and the three "city slickers" are frightened to discover they are on their own. They end up finding that one thing: they find their calling, their mission, in those obstreperous cattle.

The second of the three men has just lost his wife and his job. From the trials and tribulations of the cattle drive he learns that there is always a second chance, a new beginning, a fresh start.

The third "city slicker" never wavers in his determination to bring the herd in, even when the going gets rough. He learns the value of commitment—accepting responsibility and staying with it until the job is done.

Paradoxically, each of the three men must give up personal freedom—must give up self-indulgence, aimlessness, and self-gratification—in order to be truly free. Each must lose his life in order to find it.

That's what Paul did. And that's what you must do. Set your sights on One Thing, and move toward that goal with all your might. It is not some subjective feeling of assurance you need, it is that One Thing. Assurance is a by-product, much like happiness, of seeking God. If we pursue it directly, it proves elusive. But if we lose ourselves in loving others, both assurance and happiness will, like a butterfly, come and light on our shoulder.

But if it is unconditional assurance you're looking for, forget it. There is no such thing as unconditional assurance *even when it's based on a promise of God!* Shocking as it may seem, sometimes God has to break His promises to disobedient children.

> Therefore the Lord, the God of Israel, declares: "I promised that your house and your father's house would minister before me forever." But now the Lord declares: "Far be it from me! Those who honor me I will honor, but those who despise me will be disdained" (1 Sam. 2:30).

Ever notice that text before? God had to go back on His promise because of the unfaithfulness of Eli and his wicked sons. Here's another one:

> The angel of the Lord went up from Gilgal to Bokim and said, "I brought you up out of Egypt and led you into the land that I swore to give to your forefathers. I said, 'I will never break my covenant with you, and you shall not make a covenant with the people of this land, but you shall break down their altars.' Yet you have disobeyed me. Why have you done this? Now therefore I tell you that I will not drive them out before you; they will be thorns in your sides and their gods will be a snare to you" (Judges 2:1-3).

A third example of this is found in Numbers 14:30: "Not one of you will enter the land I swore with uplifted hand to make your home, except Caleb son of Jephunneh and Joshua son of Nun." God's most solemn promises and threatenings alike are conditional. The general principle is stated by Jeremiah:

> "O house of Israel, can I not do with you as this potter does?" declares the Lord. "Like clay in the hand of the potter, so are you in my hand, O house of Israel. If at any time I announce that a nation or kingdom is to be uprooted, torn down and destroyed, and if that nation I warned repents of its evil, then I will relent and not inflict on it the disaster I had planned. And if at another time I announce that a nation or kingdom is to be built up and planted, and if it does evil in my sight and does not obey me, then I will reconsider the good I had intended to do for it" (Jer. 18:6-10).

My mother had a saying: It is a woman's prerogative to change her mind. I don't know who came up with that idea (resistance, however, is futile). But I know this: it is certainly God's prerogative to change His mind. This idea will give any good Calvinist a conniption (another word from Mom). But God sometimes changes His preannounced plans. Besides the passages above, note 1 Chronicles 21:15 and 2 Chronicles 12:5-7. Don't ask me to explain it all logically; I just believe what Scripture says. But one reason is that everything God says has implied conditions.

Even an irrevocable promise is conditional. Romans 11:29 says that God's gifts and call are irrevocable. But they are still conditional. Irrevocable, yet conditional:

> The Lord swore an oath to David, a sure oath that he will not revoke: "One of your own descendants I will place on your throne—if your sons keep my covenant and the statutes I teach them, then their sons will sit on your throne for ever and ever" (Ps. 132:11, 12).

Here God makes an irrevocable promise to put one of David's descendants on the throne—but only if his sons are faithful to the covenant. Our continual disobedience takes us out of the realm of God's promised blessings, and our name is blotted out of the Lamb's book of life (Rev. 3:5).

God's grace is free, and abundantly available today. It's like the warm water in the shower. All we have to do is turn the tap and the water pours forth freely to envelope us in its warmth. That's how easy it is to begin the flow of grace in a life. It's not the reward of a long and costly process. Not for us anyway. The costly process was already accomplished at Calvary. All you have to do is turn the tap by inviting Him into your life. He'll take it from there. As long as we don't choke off the flow, He will complete the good work He began in us.

Friend, what is your relationship just now with this gracious and compassionate God? The past is only prologue. Things change. You are not at the mercy of some predestined fate. Up until now you may have walked all your life in God's brilliant sunshine, but you could be spending the rest of your days in the dark if you turn aside from the path of integrity.

But of course it works the other way too. You may feel like you were born under a curse. Rainclouds may follow you everywhere you go. Perhaps the ironic nickname by which your friends know you is "lucky." You or someone you know may have turned aside from the path of integrity and have excelled in evil. But history is not destiny, and the desert of your life can bud and blossom and burst into flower when God sends His rain. Repent now, and change your future. Things change. You can be a Levi.

God sent Jonah to tell wicked Ninevah that He was going to destroy it in 40 days. But it didn't happen. Ninevah changed its future by repentance. And so can you. Here is God's promise to you today: "For I know the plans I have for you," declares the Lord, "plans to prosper you and not to harm you, plans to give you hope and a future" (Jer. 29:11). "I will repay you for the years the locusts have eaten" (Joel 2:25).

Christianity is different from all other religions in this way: God's grace provides a disconnect from the past. In other religions you are at the mercy of your past. Those who are cruel in this life have bad karma, and have to work it off in some future life. But Christianity offers instant release from the load of sin. Our future is not predestined. We are not bound to the great wheel of karma. History is not destiny. Like a good computer, Christianity has a reset button. It is possible to start over and begin anew, and find our place in God's wonderful plan.

Before Osama bin Ladin was "Public Enemy No. 1" that office was occupied by Manuel Noriega, the ruthless dictator of Panama.

Noriega was captured when the United States invaded Panama in December 1989 with more than 20,000 U.S. troops. After days of being bombarded with rock music from huge speakers set up outside the Vatican embassy where he was hiding, Noriega surrendered to the U.S. Drug Enforcement Administration. The United States claimed that Noriega was paid millions by the Medellin drug cartel, headed by Pablo Escobar, to launder drug money and use Panama as a transit point for U.S.-bound drugs.

As he sat in prison early in January 1990, a copy of a Spanish New Testament came into his hands. He asked for a visit by a Christian minister. Following another visit in July 1990, Noriega enrolled in a 16-week Bible correspondence course. And another world began to open up to him.

For six months or so during 1992 Manuel Noriega was locked up in the Talledega Federal Prison in Alabama. He was kept in maximum security and allowed only one hour of freedom a day. My wife's brother, Mike Lombardo, a Seventh-day Adventist minister, was a chaplain there at the time. Mike heard that Noriega was interested in Christianity, so one day he gave him a copy of *Steps to Christ* and prayed with him. A little later Noriega asked Mike if he had any more books by Ellen G. White. So he gave him *The Desire of Ages,* and then *Christ's Object Lessons.* Noriega loved the books, and wanted more. Then he was moved back to Florida.

Eventually the former drug lord requested baptism. After a lot of legal wrangling, on October 24, 1992, General Manuel Noriega was baptized in the chambers of the Honorable William M. Hoeveler, United States District Judge, Federal Court House, Miami, Florida.

When Noriega came up out of the water, you could feel the presence of the Holy Spirit in the room, according to the Reverend Brannon who baptized him. The group sang "Amazing Grace," accompanied by an accordion. Then Noriega was allowed time for a brief testimony. He said:

> Before, Jesus to me was only an image of that which was learned from Catholicism, a historic being who worked miracles. All was transformed

when on Tuesday, January the 16th, 1990, Dr. Clift asked me in a telephone conversation, he in Texas and I in a preventive prison of the court, "Do you know that Jesus loves you?"

Today, this is what He means to me: He is the Son of God, who died on the cross for our sins, who arose from the grave and is at the right hand of God the Father and who above all things is my Savior, and has mercy on me, a sinner.

General Manuel Antonio Noriega was found guilty of international drug trafficking and sentenced to 40 years in the federal penitentiary.

One day evangelist Luis Palau visited Noriega in his Florida jail cell. Noriega told him that when he was in power in Panama, three other generals reported to him and told him of the problems their country faced. But now, he said, his kingdom was comprised of a bed, one table, and a small exercise bicycle.

Palau asked, "General, what will you do when released?" Noriega replied, "I've found a new General. When I walk out, I'll look in that Bible on my table and ask my new General what to do!"

General Manuel Antonio Noriega wrote a letter to ARM Christian Outreach International a few years ago. Here is an excerpt:

I am continuing to walk with Christ. I know everything has its season. If we humans get out of sync, everything is in trouble.

If you try to plant a crop in the middle of winter when snow is on the ground, it will not grow. Half of the problem of life is that we are constantly trying to run this schedule ourselves. But God already planned the schedule. There is an appropriate time for everything. Every morning when I arise, I repeat to myself, "God loves me, and has a wonderful plan for my body, soul, and spirit." God bless each one of you with physical health and spiritual wisdom, and please, keep up the good work.

If God can save Saul and turn him into Paul, if He can turn General Noriega into a humble Christian, then I guess He can save anyone.

CHAPTER 9

Gospel? Which Gospel?

Y ou might want to skip this chapter. It's a little bit heavy on theology, with not enough stories. But if you want to understand a lot more about the debate in the church over the last 40 years about the subject of salvation (the technical term is soteriology), then you should read it. It may answer some of the questions that have been raised by the discussion of the robe of righteousness up to this point.

Here's what I'm going to tell you: the debate between the rules-and-traditions-and-standards-and-holiness group, on the one hand, and the just-believe-and-enjoy-the-freedom-of-the-gospel group, on the other, was up and running even before the New Testament was written. And some of the apostles were on one side, some on the other. Now that sounds kind of interesting, doesn't it?

Down through the centuries seekers after God have asked, What is the gospel? The word gospel means "good news," and the term originates in Isaiah (40:9; 41:27; 52:7). Exactly what does the gospel include? It focuses on the facts of Jesus' life, death, and resurrection in fulfillment of the Old Testament prophecies (Rom. 1:1ff.; 1 Cor. 15:1ff.; 2 Tim. 2:8) and all of the ensuing consequences. As Jesus is Lord, He is also Judge, and hence the doctrine of the final judgment is part of the gospel (Rom. 2:16; Rev. 14:6, 7). The gospel not only looks backward, it also looks forward, since the kingdom of God is not yet consummated. Thus Colossians 1:22, 23 says Christ has reconciled the Colossian Christians to present them "holy in his sight, without blemish and free from accusation—if you continue in your faith, established and firm, not moved from the hope held out in the gospel" which he has earlier defined as "the hope that is stored up for you in heaven" (verse 5). Thus the gospel includes the good news of the coming kingdom:

> Jesus went into Galilee, proclaiming the good news of God. "The time has come," he said. "The kingdom of God is near. Repent and believe the good news" (Mark 1:14, 15).

Here's what's interesting about this passage: it tells us that the "gospel" in Jesus' day meant the good news of the coming kingdom of God. It included nothing about the life, death, and resurrection of Christ, which was still future at the time. And this message included a call to repent. Those who claim that the gospel is solely about the "doing and dying of Jesus" are somewhat wide of the mark.

The "eternal gospel" of Revelation 14:6, 7 includes the command to "fear God and give him glory." Second Thessalonians 1:8 and 1 Peter 4:17 speak of "those who do not obey the gospel," clearly implying that the gospel is not only indicative but imperative—that is, it demands action in the present, it is not merely a set of facts about something that happened in the past. Obedience to the message of the gospel is possible because the gospel is a life-changing power (1 Thess. 1:5ff.; Rom. 15:16); it is "the power of God for the salvation of everyone who believes" (Rom. 1:16). And it involves ethical norms: First Timothy 1:8-11 lists various vices which are "contrary to the sound doctrine that conforms to the glorious gospel of the blessed God." So the gospel says not only "done," but also "do."

That's what the New Testament says about the gospel. But the very question "What is the gospel?" is misleading in this way: the term "gospel" is basically Paul's term. Even after we have decided exactly what Paul meant by it, it is still one inspired writer's take on the Christian message. Other New Testament writers rarely use the term. John wrote more of the New Testament than Paul, and he wrote after Paul did, yet John uses the term "gospel" (Greek *euangelion/euangelia*) just once (Rev. 14:6). His term for the Christian message is "truth" (Greek *aletheia*) and "testimony/witness" (Greek *marturia*), and his version of that message has a different flavor, and different emphases, from that of Paul.

In other words when you hear two Christians having a theological debate, and one cries "truth," while the other cries "gospel," you can know them by their shibboleths. They may not realize it, but you are hearing an argument between Johannine and Pauline theology.

Back in the 1980s some evangelical Adventist dreamed up the label "TOADs" (Traditional Old ADventists) versus FROGs (FRiends Of the Gospel). I am suggesting that these two groups can be traced *right back into the New Testament.*

Paul was a FROG, along with Barnabas and Luke. Peter and John, and James and Jude (older half-brothers of Jesus), and probably the rest of the twelve, were basically TOADS.

Notice that the two most "evangelical" parables in the gospels, the Pharisee and the publican, and the prodigal son, are found only in the Gospel composed by Luke, Paul's assistant. (If you're wondering about another gospel-oriented parable, the woman taken in adultery, its location is not fixed in the Greek manuscripts—believe it or not, it wanders around from Gospel to Gospel!). So Luke's theology tends to be FROGish. Luke, though, was something of a mediator: there seems to be a conscious attempt in Acts to balance the accounts of miracles by Paul with similar accounts of miracles by Peter.

Here is another way to think about the matter. Traditional Adventist soteriology tends to be derived from the Epistles at the end of the Bible, James through Revelation (known as the General or Catholic Epistles). Evangelical soteriology tends to be drawn from the letters of Paul.

We find all the flavors of theology in the writings of Ellen G. White, of course, since she drew from all of those sources.

Let's take a closer look at some of these sources. James the brother of Jesus was a TOAD if ever there was one. He was a teetotaler and a vegetarian, known among the conservatives of Jerusalem (i.e., Pharisees) for his piety. Hegesippus says James was "holy from his mother's womb, and he drank no wine nor strong drink, nor did he eat flesh" (Eusebius, *Histories* 2.23.5). Paul, on the other hand, seems to have had alternative opinions on diet (Rom. 14:6, 14, 20-22; 1 Cor. 10:25; 1 Tim. 4:3). The evidence suggests that James, pious traditionalist and church administrator, did not always see eye to eye with Paul, maverick and scholar, even on some more fundamental issues.

Things haven't changed much in 2,000 years, have they?

A dispute arose in the early church about whether a new convert had to be circumcised to be saved—a classical TOAD/FROG confrontation. The "General Conference brethren" called a meeting to discuss the matter in Jerusalem, and the Holy Spirit guided them to a consensus. Their decision is stated in Acts 15:29: "You are to abstain from food sacrificed to idols, from blood, from the meat of strangled animals and from sexual immorality." This decision applied only to Gentile converts (verses 19, 23); Jewish Christians were still expected to keep the whole law.

The logical and scriptural basis of this decision is not obvious, because it is not mentioned in the account we have. What happened is that the church decided to require Gentile Christians to keep only those parts of the ceremonial law which the Torah says apply to *proselytes*, the New Testament term for Jewish converts who are not Jews by birth. The four stipulations are a summary of the things forbidden to *proselytes* in Leviticus 17 and 18, LXX. (Keep in mind, by the way, that the ongoing validity of the Ten Commandments is assumed and never discussed at this meeting. Obviously the church leaders did not decide that it was okay from now on for Christians to take the Lord's name in vain, worship idols, kill, steal, or break the Sabbath—particularly since the Sabbath is also explicitly said to apply to *proselytes* in Exodus 20:10, LXX.)

However, Paul may have been somewhat uncomfortable with parts of this agreement. In 1 Corinthians 8-10 he tends to create a few loopholes in the rules prohibiting food offered to idols.

A few years later, when Paul last visited Jerusalem, we find evidence of continuing tension between him and James. This disagreement is apparent if one reads closely between the lines of the conversation between Paul and James recorded in Acts 21:18-25. Verse 25 is the key. "But as for the Gentile believers [not Jewish believers], we have written to them that they should abstain from food sacrificed to idols, from blood, from the meat of strangled animals and from sexual immorality."

In other words James is rebuking Paul for teaching *Jewish* Christians who live among the Gentiles that they are no longer bound by the stipulations of the ceremonial law. This is exactly what Paul is accused of teaching in verse 21. But that would be contrary to the decision reached by the leaders in Acts 15, which had nothing to do with Jewish Christians at all. Only *Gentile* Christians were exempted from the law. In other words the church leaders were reminding Paul that the entire ceremonial law was still in force for Jewish believers. The leaders suggest that Paul show his submission to the law by joining a group of Jews carrying out the Nazirite vow (the rules of which are found in Numbers 6), which Paul then proceeds to do (Acts 21:26).

More evidence of a rift between Paul and James is the fact that the group against which Paul directs his Epistle to the Galatians seem to have been emissaries of James (Gal. 2:12; cf. 5:1-12)—or at least that is how they represented themselves to Paul.

The differences between Paul and James go deeper than the question of diet or circumcision. Modern conservative scholars have gone to great pains to show that Paul in Romans and James are standing back to back, fighting opposite errors. The Epistle of James, they say, is not correcting Paul's teaching, but a perversion of it.

Well . . .

In chapter 2 of his Epistle James argues against the formula "faith alone." He seems to be uncomfortable with some of the implications of Paul's argument for righteousness by faith in Romans 3 and 4. This becomes obvious when we lay Rom. 3:28, "We maintain that a man is justified by faith apart from observing the law," alongside James 2:24, "You see that a person is justified by what he does and not by faith alone." Sounds like a difference of opinion to me.

Now there are several ways to harmonize these passages; one is to distinguish works of law from works of faith (Gal. 5:6). Another is to distinguish between initial and final justification. Still, though, the phrase "by faith alone" occurs only here in the Greek New Testament—*where it is rejected as error.* And it is no accident that both writers appeal to the very same Old Testament proof text about Abraham to arrive at very different conclusions (cp. James 2:21-23 with Romans 4:1-5).

Does this mean that we have two different gospels in the New Testament? No. There is an underlying harmony. But although they agreed on the fundamentals of faith in Christ, and that Christ was the only way of salvation, and that His death on the cross provided the solution for sin, I think James and Paul had differences of opinion. Ellen White thought so too:

> Paul held to his inspired truth, and taught it to others, opposed as he was by the apostles, who ought to have upheld him. . . . Paul's brethren withstood him. Those whom the Lord had used as His witnesses protested against him, and declared that he was advocating theories that were contrary to the fundamental principles which they had been taught. But Paul firmly held his ground (*Review and Herald,* May 25, 1897).

In other words, even inspired writers sometimes suspect other inspired writers of heresy!

Where did Peter stand in this dispute? Second Peter 3:16, 17 provides a clue. Here Peter says that Paul's writings are hard to understand and easy to misinterpret (3:16), then immediately warns against antinomianism (3:17). Peter is clearly on the traditionalist side. Does this shed some light on the falling out between Peter and Paul mentioned in Galatians 2:11-14?

Jude the brother of Jesus also opposes antinomianism. He writes against "godless men, who change the grace of our God into a license for immorality" (verse 4). Surely he is not talking about Paul, but he may be talking about some of Paul's unbalanced disciples.

The case of John is the most interesting of all. John is certainly an evangelical. He speaks of Christ as our atoning sacrifice (1 John 2:2), and says that if we sin, we have an advocate with the Father (1 John 2:1). "If we claim to be without sin," writes John, "we deceive ourselves" (1 John 1:8). While John emphasizes keeping the commandments, he says that the command of Jesus we should be keeping is to believe on the name of the Lord Jesus Christ (1 John 3:22, 23). A believer may know that he has eternal life (1 John 5:13).

But John comes down mostly on the TOAD side of the equation. He strongly upholds the apostolic decrees of Acts 15 in his letters to the seven churches, condemning those groups in the church that ignored them (Rev. 2:14, 20). It is still essential, he says, to abstain from meat offered to idols. That he has the apostolic decree in mind is indicated by his allusion to Acts 15:28 in Revelation 2:24, "I place no other burden upon you."

In the writings of John righteousness is never "imputed," "as if," or forensic. Righteousness is defined as rightdoing: "He who does what is right is righteous, just as he is righteous" (1 John 3:7); "If you know that he is righteous, you know that everyone who does what is right has been born of him" (1 John 2:29). "This is how we know we are in him: whoever claims to live in him must walk as Jesus did" (1 John 2:5, 6). John says the reason our prayers are answered is because we are obedient (1 John 3:22). Christians born of God do not continue to sin (1 John 3:5-10). "When he appears, we shall be like him. . . . Everyone who has this hope in him purifies himself, just as he is pure" (1 John 3:2, 3). John emphasizes separation from the world (1 John 2:15-17).

John is a Puritan. Unlike the rest of the apostles he never married; the unanimous testimony of the early church fathers is that John was a lifelong virgin. (Epiphanius, *Panarion* Haer. 78.10, 13, 58.4; Jerome, *Adversus Jovinianum* 1.26; Augustine, *Tractatus in Evangelium Joannis* 124.7). With this in mind, read his description of the 144,000 in Revelation 14:1-5. Notice also how John speaks of Christian holiness as an unsoiled robe:

> You have a few people in Sardis who have not soiled their clothes. They will walk with me, dressed in white, for they are worthy. He who overcomes will, like them, be dressed in white. I will never blot out his name from the book of life, but will acknowledge his name before my Father and his angels (Rev. 3:4-5).

To sum up John's theology, the robe of character must be unsoiled. If it is soiled, it must be washed white in the blood of the Lamb.

Even Paul, the great apostle of grace, who defines the term gospel, is not "evangelical" enough for some who insist on the crucial importance of the distinction between imputed (external) and imparted (internal) righteousness. Like John, Paul exhorts his readers to purify themselves and to perfect holiness (2 Cor. 7:1) so they will be found blameless at the coming of Christ (1 Thess. 3:13; 5:23, 24; cp. 2 Peter 3:14). Following his presentation of righteousness by faith in Romans, Paul writes that those who live according to the flesh must die (Rom. 8:13). Following his presentation of the gospel in Galatians, Paul writes that anyone who is living an immoral life will not inherit the kingdom (Gal. 5:19-21). This must be important to Paul because he makes the very same point in two other letters: anyone practicing vices A, B, C, D, or E will not inherit the kingdom of God (1 Cor. 6:9, 10; Eph. 5:5). Paul is as strong on the need for personal holiness as any writer of Scripture.

Paul contends that salvation is a free gift, and not a *misthos*—a word that means "pay, wages, reward, recompense" (Rom. 4:4, 5; 5:15-18; 6:23; 2 Cor. 9:15; Eph. 2:8). Yet a broad spectrum of New Testament writers, *including Paul,* do not hesitate to speak of the final *misthos* of the believer (Matt. 5:12; 10:41f.; 16:27; Luke 6:23; 1 Cor. 3:8; Col. 3:24; Heb. 10:35; 11:26; 2 John 8; Rev. 22:12). Salvation is a free gift, yet it involves a reward.

One of the results of Christ's death, according to Romans 8:4, is that "the righteous requirements of the law might be fully met *in us*"—note, not "in Christ for us"—"who do not live according to the sinful nature but according to the Spirit." Titus 3:5 says we are saved by the washing of regeneration and renewing of the Holy Spirit, and Paul makes a similar statement in 2 Thessalonians 2:13. Paul sounds very much like James when he writes, "It is not those who hear the law who are righteous in God's sight, but it is those who obey the law who will be declared righteous" (Rom. 2:13). Paul sums up his own message this way: "First to those in Damascus, then to those in Jerusalem and in all Judea, and to the Gentiles also, I preached that they should repent and turn to God and prove their repentance by their deeds" (Acts 26:20).

The New Testament consistently teaches that believers will be judged as worthy (Luke 20:35, 36; 2 Thess. 1:5; Rev. 3:4) or unworthy of salvation by their works (Matt. 16:27; 25:31-46; John 5:28, 29; Rom. 2:6-11; 2 Cor. 5:10; 1 Pet.1:17; Rev. 22:12). On this point the apostles speak with one voice. Nowhere in Scripture do we find the idea that in the final judgment Christ's works are judged in place of the believer's works. Nor is the judgment only to determine the degree of reward, for Romans 2:6-11 and John 5:29 make it clear that we are judged by works for salvation or damnation. Saved by grace, judged by works. This is the clear teaching of Scripture from Genesis to Revelation.

This does not even rise to the level of a paradox; it is something we can understand from customs around us today. Newly purchased cars in most states must be inspected before they can be driven. Cars that fail the test are sent back to the mechanic. The testers do not fix the car, the mechanic does. The car is judged by its performance, but "saved" by the mechanic. Similarly, the law is our schoolmaster to send us to Christ. It is Christ, not the law, that saves. Saved by grace, judged by works. The works only serve to test the genuineness of the faith.

Please note that no passage of Scripture suggests that it is impossible to keep the law. Paul states that it is the *carnal* man who cannot keep the law, then goes on to contrast the situation of the spiritual man (Rom. 8:6–9). Paul and John both claim that we have all sinned (Rom. 3:23; 1 John 1:8, 10), but that is not the same thing as saying that God's rules cannot be kept. Both Paul and James are quite clear that Christians who know the law will be judged by the law of the Ten Commandments (Rom. 2:12–16; James 2:10–12).

Unfortunately, those who shy away from antinomianism often fall into the opposite ditch of perfectionism. Perfectionism involves the idea that unless one is keeping the law to the nth degree, one is not keeping it at all. Neither Jesus' Sermon on the Mount or James 2:10 justifies this conclusion. The same God who gave His children practical commands also gives us the spiritual power to keep them. Holy living never implies absolute sinless perfection. This mistake, which is made by both sides, leads to extreme conclusions: either absolute sinless perfection is essential for salvation, or else the only righteousness human beings can have is forensic. Neither conclusion is correct. The righteousness Scripture speaks of is not some end point beyond which there can be no further progress, but a realizable state of loving obedience to God that is available to all.

The New Testament provides actual examples of individuals who were living blameless lives. Zechariah, for example, was "upright in the sight of God, observing all the Lord's commandments and regulations blamelessly" or "perfectly" (Luke 1:6). Yet when Zechariah was confronted with a higher test (Luke 1:18–20) involving a command which was "outside the system," he failed the test. Human beings can achieve flawlessness only within a certain limited and defined sphere. It is not *sinless* living but *holy* living that is the privilege of every child of God.

It can never be repeated often enough, of course, that works are only the condition, never the ground or basis, for salvation. The only ground of our salvation is a vicarious atonement, a substitutionary sacrifice so that the perfect righteousness of Jesus' life may be credited to us as a gift. No amount of righteous living can entitle any soul to heaven. Every sinner deserves to die for his sin, regardless of how flawless a life they may live after conversion. Only grace can grant eternal life.

The notion that we are saved by our good works is heresy. So is the evangelical notion that our works have nothing to do with our salvation. Saying that works have nothing to do with salvation is like saying that the thermometer reading has nothing to do with the temperature. It is essential to maintain the New Testament tension between the necessity of good works and the all-sufficiency of grace.

I know of no better passage to illustrate this tension than Hebrews 10, which contains arguably the strongest assurance passage, and the strongest unassurance passage, in all of Scripture.

> We have been made holy through the sacrifice of the body of Jesus Christ once for all . . . because by one sacrifice he has made perfect forever those who are being made holy. . . . Since we have a great priest over the house of God, let us draw near to God with a sincere heart in full assurance of faith (Heb. 10:10, 14, 21, 22).

Now that's assurance! The sin problem has been taken care of. We have been made perfect once and for all forever.

Yet only a few verses later the same author states, "If we deliberately keep on sinning after we have received the knowledge of the truth, no sacrifice for sins is left" (Heb. 10:26). "Without holiness no one will see the Lord" (Heb. 12:14).

Did you feel a little stab of anxiety just now? That anxiety is a good thing. If you don't understand why, go back and read chapters 7 and 8. Psychologists tell us that a positive motivation works better than a negative one—a promise of reward works better than a threat of loss. But, they claim, what works even better are positive and negative motivations used together. That's right: the carrot and the stick work better than the carrot alone. God, who formed our minds, knew all about this before the psychologists figured it out decades ago. That's why He holds out the promise of heaven and the threat of hell, because we need all the motivation we can get!

In the end it's all about the cross. We do not live a holy life to gain salvation, but because we are saved. Striving for holiness of life is not, however, optional. Those who have died by the cross ("one died for all, therefore all died") have the privilege of living by the cross, of bearing the cross for Jesus. Those who boldly preach God's free justifying grace apart from the works of the law have something potent to offer the world: not an impotent gospel that begins and ends with legal fictions, but one that provides the power to "purify ourselves from everything that contaminates body and spirit, and perfecting holiness out of reverence for God" (2 Cor. 7:1). Our goal is to channel God's grace to the world, becoming God's hands and feet and voices to bring lost humanity to Jesus Christ.

The idea of theological differences between Paul and the twelve, between Hellenistic Christianity and Jewish Christianity, has been discussed by generations of scholars; it is certainly no original observation of mine. God took all of these viewpoints and put them together in the same Bible. And it is Scripture as a whole that is the standard. Adventists have always rejected the idea of a canon within the canon. There is no external rule, prior to and higher than the canon, by which we may hold up one inspired writer as more authoritative than another. Part of the genius of the Seventh-day Adventist faith is that it calls into play the whole panoply of scriptural truth, not merely some carefully selected subset of it.

Even the concept of progressive revelation must be used with care, since one of the attributes of God is that He does not change. The "canon within a canon" crowd usually elevates the writings of Paul to special status. But if the latest New Testament writer is the most authoritative, then the writings of John would have the highest authority, wouldn't they? The point is that we run into problems whenever we say that one New Testament writer is somehow more "authoritative" than another.

If we find it hard to fit all of the apostolic teachings into a single, harmonious system, then perhaps the problem lies with our system and its faulty hidden assumptions. But the doctrine of salvation is no different than many other aspects of reality. Is an elephant more like a rope, a pillar, or a wall? It depends on which part of the elephant you are holding at the moment. Is light a wave or a particle? The strange answer, physicists tell us, is yes—and, believe me, modern physics gets much, much stranger than this!

I love the cover photograph on Douglas Hofstadter's Pulitzer-prize-winning book, *Godel, Escher, Bach: An Eternal Golden Braid*. There a complex three-dimensional object suspended in space casts three different shadows on three different walls. The walls stand at right angles to each other as in the corner of any ordinary room. The first shadow assumes the shape of a capital E. On the second wall, at right angles to the first, is a G. The third shadow is a B. The shape that casts these disparate shadows is a single, complex physical object created on shop equipment.

The gospel is like that. Paul and James and John are looking at the same central truth from different vantage points. All of their viewpoints are different ways of understanding the whole.

Truth is a symphony. It is a rich chiaroscuro of part and counterpart, thesis and antithesis, with many different players, moving through transient discord into perfect harmony. We must resist the temptation to reduce the Biblical symphony to one tune, disallowing the more strident contrasting motifs that give the symphony depth and texture, so that only the first violin may be heard, playing over and over the same refrain. This reductionism is a serious problem in some forms of evangelical Protestantism. Let us never surrender to it.

The apostles are, in fact, all reading from the same score; they are playing the same symphony under the direction of the Master Composer. There are not several different gospels in the New Testament; only one. But it is broad, deep, and rich enough to reveal its mystery in a new way to every seeking heart.

CHAPTER 10

Dressed for the King

I was having a lovely Sabbath dinner at the house of some delightful friends when they told me this story: before Bill asked Laura to marry him, he asked her if she wanted a wedding ring.

No, she said, she'd rather spend that sort of money on something like, oh, say, building a church in Honduras, than wasting it on a wedding band.

What a capital idea! So that's what they did. In August 1999 they built a church in La Lima, Honduras. It cost them about the same as they would have spent on a millennial platinum wedding band, which some of their friends were buying. At the end of the 10-day building project, to which many others contributed, the church had a baptism, a communion, and a wedding. Their own. The whole town turned out for it.

What a wonderful story! Here's a more sobering one.

A recently baptized member, full of new zeal, came into contact with a "sophisticated" Adventist who saw no problem with wearing jewelry. When the new convert asked about it, she said something like, "My salvation doesn't depend on jewelry." As a result, the new convert started wearing jewelry.

I hear this comment now and again in various forms. It strikes me as one of the most childish things a Christian can say. My salvation may not depend on my diet, either, but that is no argument against healthful living. The question "Is it essential to my salvation" is a sure sign of an immature Christian. Imagine a father telling his daughter, "Please don't scuff your shoes," and the daughter replying, "Will you throw me out of the house if I do?"

I wonder how God must feel when his children ask how much they can get away with without losing their salvation.

A Christian is always trying to find out what pleases the Lord (Eph. 5:10), not asking whether this or that is absolutely necessary for "my salvation." Since when is my salvation the most important thing? Is it really all about me? What about God's preferences? What might advance His goals? What might make Him happy?

My marriage does not really depend on whether I buy my wife roses, or give in to her choice of restaurants for today. But I have discovered that when I give up something for her, I'm not really losing out on something, I'm getting in on something!

Well, that goes double-scotch googol-plenty for God.

A googol, by the way, is a very big number. It's a 1 followed by 100 zeros. The name was invented by a mathematician in 1938 long before Google, the all-knowing Web site, existed. The site was named after the number by someone who was better at math than spelling. (Just for your amusement: the only larger number with a name is a googolplex, which is a one with a googol zeroes after it. Just writing out the number using any normal sized font would fill the known universe. But I digress.)

Here's something to think about when we encounter a rule without explanation: maybe God knows something we don't. God may have a googol reasons for suggesting that jewelry does not suit His preferences.

Here's one that has occurred to me, for what it's worth. Maybe gemstones are worn in heaven as insignias of rank, and God would prefer that His children observe the heavenly protocol, and not impersonate an officer by wearing insignia that doesn't belong to them. That may sound kind of zany, but it is suggested to me by Ezekiel 28:13, 14:

> You were in Eden, the garden of God; every precious stone adorned you: ruby, topaz and emerald, chrysolite, onyx and jasper, sapphire, turquoise and beryl. Your settings and mountings were made of gold; on the day you were created they were prepared. You were anointed as a guardian cherub, for so I ordained you. You were on the holy mount of God; you walked among the fiery stones.

The "settings and mountings" mentioned here, by the way, are terms any jeweler would understand; they have nothing to do with musical instruments—an idea based on a misunderstanding of the KJV translation "tabrets and pipes." The point is that Lucifer was bedecked with jewelry. In his prepride state, before he fell, he had a right.

Come to think of it, jewels are also insignias of rank worn by the high priest. Read the description of his bejeweled and gilded breastplate in Exodus 28. So there is nothing inherently evil about jewelry at all. Jewels are bestowed by heaven as emblems of honor, rank, and status. Perhaps that's the problem. I wonder if perhaps the inhabitants of heaven don't feel the same way about God's children wearing jewelry that the United States Army feels about a private putting on the stars of a general.

Perhaps another principle here is the image of God. What would we think of someone who desecrated one of Leonardo DaVinci's fine paintings? The human body is God's great work of art. Certain things are a defacement of the image of God, such as bodily tattoos, which are forbidden in Leviticus 19:28. And why on earth would a woman want to look like someone had given her a black eye? On the other hand cosmetic strategies which tend to restore the image of God, such as wigs for the bald or natural makeup to hide facial blemishes, are surely no violation of principle.

Certain kinds of dress symbolize certain lifestyles. The early Christian church was, among other things, an antiluxury movement. Surely the antiluxury principle would apply to expensive furs, expensive cars, expensive vases, etc. But the *symbol* for the lifestyle that is explicitly prescribed in the Word of God is a lack of personal adornment. An absence of bling.

Many organizations have certain insignias or distinctive garments that are worn with pride. The Shriners wear a red hat known as a fez. Observant Jews wear a skullcap or yarmulke. Brides wear veils. Those who join the armed forces wear their uniforms with pride. Imagine a potential Shriner, invited to join the organization, saying, "I admire and respect the ideals of this organization, and I want to be a part of it, but I just can't bring myself to wear that funny little red hat!"

The prohibition of jewelry is an ancient tradition. The pilgrims who founded our nation didn't wear jewelry. Many churches used to exclude jewelry. Adventists have traditionally abstained from earrings, necklaces, or rings with the exception of the wedding ring. Today some seem embarrassed with this tradition. But the reason the issue is still alive is because of certain New Testament passages that seem to take a low view of high fashion.

Let's start with the Old Testament. Stripping off jewelry is associated with revival and reform in the Torah (Gen. 35:1-5; Ex. 33:5, 6). Facial paint is also discouraged. The practice of painting the eyes with vivid blue eye shadow is an ancient custom that was widely practiced in ancient Egypt when the Israelites were slaves there. It is mentioned three times in the Old Testament, and in each case it is associated with prostitution (2 Kings 9:30; Jer. 4:30; Eze. 23:40). These and other passages (Isa. 3:16-24; Hos. 2:13; Rev. 17:4; 18:16) also associate jewelry with a certain kind of woman.

This is a transcultural thing: such dress bears the same connotation to this day. The next time you watch a movie, notice how an actor dresses to play a prostitute. People who are empty inside seem to need extra ornamentation outside, and human nature doesn't change much from age to age.

There are some Old Testament passages that mention jewelry in a neutral sense. But the New Testament position on dress, like that on divorce, is even more conservative than the Old. The bride of Christ is dressed in fine linen, bright and clean (Rev. 19:8)—the dress worn by the ascetic community at Qumran that produced the Dead Sea Scrolls—while the whore of Babylon wears expensive fashions aglitter with gold, precious stones, and pearls (Rev. 17:4; 18:16; cf. Luke 16:19). The two most important passages are from Peter and Paul, apostles who both suffered martyrdom about the same time at Rome.

> I also want women to dress modestly, with decency and propriety, not with braided hair or gold or pearls or expensive clothes, but with good deeds, appropriate for women who profess to worship God (1 Tim. 2:9, 10).

> Your beauty should not come from outward adornment, such as braided hair and the wearing of gold jewelry and fine clothes. Instead, it should be that of your inner self, the unfading beauty of a gentle and quiet spirit, which is of great worth in God's sight (1 Pet. 3:3, 4).

This formula, "not X, but Y," occurs dozens of times in the New Testament. The X is something to be rejected, while Y is affirmed. In other words, "not X, but Y" does *not* mean "not *only* X, but *also* Y" (when Paul wants to say that, he includes the words "only" and "also" in the Greek text). Examples of the "not X, but Y" formula include 1 Corinthians 4:20, "For the kingdom of God is not a matter of talk but of power;" or 14:33, "For God is not a God of disorder but of peace;" or Titus 2:3, "not to be slanderers or addicted to much wine, but to teach what is good;" or 2:10, "not to steal from them, but to show that they can be fully trusted;" or 3:5, "not because of righteous things we had done, but because of his mercy;" or 2 Timothy 1:7, "For God did not give us a spirit of timidity, but a spirit of power, of love and of self-discipline," etc. Paul's and Peter's statements about jewelry are examples of this "not X, but Y" formula. Elaborate hairstyles (which involved spending most of a day in the salon for upper class Roman women), fine clothing, and gold jewelry are ruled out for the Christian.

Peter and Paul here are standing in a certain line of Jewish puritan tradition. Other Jewish writers—Greek and Roman too—make similar points. Take Philo, a Jewish philosopher living in Alexandria at the same time Jesus lived in Galilee. In his book *On the Birth of Abel* (5.21) he speaks of a woman who "comes to us luxuriously dressed in the guise of a harlot and prostitute, with mincing steps, . . . having the hair of her head dressed with most superfluous elaborateness, having her eyes pencilled, her eyebrows covered over, using incessant warm baths, painted with a fictitious color, exquisitely dressed with costly garments, richly embroidered, adorned with armlets, and bracelets, and necklaces, and all other ornaments which can be made of gold, and precious stones, and all kinds of female decorations; . . . out of the scarcity of any genuine beauty, pursuing a bastard elegance."

One piece of literature the apostles may have read was the *Testament of the Twelve Patriarchs.* One not atypical passage is *Testament of Reuben* 5:4, 5, "My children, flee from sexual promiscuity, and order your wives and your daughters not to adorn their heads and their appearances so as to deceive men's sound minds. For every woman who schemes in these ways is destined for eternal punishment."

That is the trajectory just prior to the writing of the New Testament. What about the trajectory just afterward? How did the early church understand these passages on jewelry?

Around A.D. 200 Clement was the senior pastor of the church at Alexandria. He wrote the lyrics to the oldest hymn in Christian hymnody, "Shepherd of Tender Youth." It was Clement who recorded the amazing story of the apostle John's pursuit of the lapsed youth found in an earlier chapter of this book. Clement was a prolific writer. He wrote a manual for baptismal candidates called *The Instructor.* In it he explained why Christian women should not wear luxurious clothes, or elaborate hair styles, or "smear their faces." Concerning earrings, he wrote, "The Word prohibits us from doing violence to nature by boring the lobes of the ears. For why not the nose, too?" He allowed one functional ring, not for ornament, but for use as a seal.

In other words, one hundred years after the close of the New Testament, Clement interpreted those New Testament passages on jewelry in exactly the same way as Adventists do: only a modest piece of *functional* jewelry is allowed.

Tertullian's treatise *On the Apparel of Women* is a lively pointed attack on contemporary Roman fashion. Tertullian encouraged Christian women to forego elaborate forms of clothing, jewelry, hairstyle, and cosmetics.

The *Apostolic Constitutions,* a late fourth-century collection of church law, outlawed the use of all finger rings: "Neither put a gold ring upon your fingers; for all these ornaments are signs of lasciviousness."

The Adventist tradition is in line with late pre-Christian, Christian, and postapostolic teaching on jewelry.

Abstaining from jewelry is no doubt less important than most other topics mentioned in the Bible, but Jesus said in Luke 11:42: "Woe to you Pharisees, because you give God a tenth of your mint, rue and all other kinds of garden herbs, but you neglect justice and the love of God. You should have practiced the latter *without leaving the former undone.*" In other words there are more important matters, and less important ones (like jewelry). But everything has its place.

Sometimes little things are very important, revealing the loyalties of the heart. Those who think personal adornment hardly worth discussing must surely deplore the narrowmindedness of certain religious enthusiasts who would risk life and limb rather than tie their shoes at a convenient moment in front of Nebuchadnezzar's golden image, or put a simple pinch of incense on Caesar's altar. In an age when millions were dying of hunger or cruelty, how could such picayune, ritualistic trivialities come to be considered an ultimate test of faith?

Yet they were. Great crises of faith often come down to ritualistic issues—such as which day is the Sabbath. Just as a flag is more than a dyed piece of cloth, and incense is more than a chemical, so there is a symbolic issue involved in the wearing of jewelry which transcends the question of its actual expense.

The song of the surrendered soul is, "All to Jesus I surrender, all to Him I freely give!" At that point sacrifice becomes a pleasure. But the change must come from the inside and work its way out. Forcing oneself to take off jewelry that is still the darling of the heart will bring misery. Only when the heart is yielded, and we are willing to allow God to lay our glory in the dust, will joy shine through and the jewelry fall off.

"Your attitude," writes Paul in Phillipians 2, "should be the same as that of Christ Jesus: who, being in very nature God, did not consider equality with God something to be grasped, but made himself nothing." If Jesus could lay aside His rightful crown and wealth and live among us as a poor peasant, and then die as a criminal, so that we might have His riches, surely there is nothing too large for us to give up for Him.

Remember: "Always be trying to find out what best pleases the Lord" (see Eph. 5:10). When we give up something for God, we are not losing out on something. We are getting in on something. God has a googol of blessings in store for those who ask, "Lord, how better can I please you?"

An old book entitled *Deeper Experiences of Famous Christians* details the lives of several great men and women of God whose lives have blessed millions. I was amazed to learn how many of them went through a dark period in their life when they felt separated from the Lord—a period that often lasted not weeks or months but years.

One such person was Frances Ridley Havergal (1836-1879). She was the youngest child of an Anglican pastor. She began to write verse at the age of 7, and later learned a number of languages, both ancient and modern. She was a brilliant pianist and loved to sing, but she sang only sacred songs. At the age of 14 she committed her soul to God, and she wrote "earth and heaven seemed brighter from that moment." She was very close to the Lord in her youth. At 22 years of age she had memorized all of the Gospels, Epistles, Revelation, Psalms, and Isaiah by heart.

Havergal became known as a religious writer, with a fine gift for poetry. She sought the Lord with all her heart. Her mind was so saturated with the Scriptures that her hymns are a mosaic of scriptural phrases. Of her hymn-writing she wrote, "Writing is praying with me, for I never seem to write even a verse by myself. I ask that at every line He would give me, not merely thoughts and power, but also every word, even the very rhymes. Very often I have a most distinct consciousness of direct answers."

Nevertheless, there came a time in her life more than 15 years long when she felt a lack of true spiritual peace. She lived, she said, in "sunless ravines" She wondered why others obtained the blessing so easily that she had agonized and prayed for so long.

But find it she did, suddenly on December 2, 1873, after reading a book called "All For Jesus" sent by a friend. Suddenly the sun broke through in her life. Shortly thereafter she wrote a hymn. It happened in this way. In February of 1874 Frances paid a five-day visit to Arely House, in Londer, where ten other persons were staying. They were all either unconverted or unhappy, and Miss Havergal was impressed to pray for them so that they might all have the joy she had. Her prayer was, "Lord, give me ALL in this house."

The night before her departure, the last two young ladies surrendered after a personal visit from Miss Havergal. By that time it was nearly midnight, but the answer to her prayer made her so happy that she could not sleep, and the words to a poem came to her and she wrote it down. "Take my life, and let it be consecrated, Lord, to Thee. . . . Take my voice, and let me sing always, only, for my King. . . . Take myself, and I will be, ever, only, all for Thee."

The hymn did not appear in print until 1878, four years later. When Miss Havergal first read the second stanza in print—"Take my silver and my gold, not a mite would I withhold"—she was suddenly convicted of her own failure to do just that, for she had an exquisite collection of jewelry, most by gift or inheritance, kept in an unusually fine jewel cabinet.

She immediately packed the jewel box full and sent it to her church missionary society to be sold for funds.

"I have never packed a box with such pleasure," she later exclaimed.

CHAPTER 11

Friends in High Places

Let us now praise Bach.

Whether the angels play only Bach praising God, I am not quite sure.
—Karl Barth

Bach is Bach, as God is God.
—Hector Berlioz

To give wings of eternity to that which is most ephemeral; to make divine things human and human things divine; such is Bach, the greatest and purest moment in music of all time.
—Pablo Casals

Bach is like an astronomer who, with the help of ciphers, finds the most wonderful stars.
—Friederick Chopin

The greatest Christian music in the world. . . . If life had taken hope and faith from me, this single chorus would restore all.
—Felix Mendelssohn

Bach is the beginning and end of all music.
 —Max Reger

All modern music owes everything to Bach.
 —Nikolai Rimsky-Korsakov

The biologist and philosopher Lewis Thomas was asked what record of human achievements he would launch into space to be discovered one day by some transgalactic civilization. Thomas suggested a continual broadcast of Bach—though, he said, "that would be boasting."

But we can do much better than that, as even Bach himself—a Christian—would tell us.

If Bach is the greatest musician, then who is the greatest advocate, the greatest mediator, the greatest intercessor, of all time?

Well, the answer is so extreme that we need to work up to it.

Let's start by going back to the days of the American Revolution. In the town of Ephrata, Pennsylvania, a man by the name of Michael Whitman or Widman owned a hotel. Whitman was an outspoken Tory who opposed the Revolution. He also served as a board member of the Reformed Church.

Less than a mile from Whitman's inn lived Peter Miller, who had abandoned the Reformed Church to become the leader of the Ephrata Cloister, a group of German Seventh-day Baptists who practiced celibacy and kept the Sabbath. Miller spoke many languages. Benjamin Franklin asked him on behalf of the Continental Congress to translate the Declaration of Independence into seven languages so it could be sent to foreign powers.

Now Michael Whitman hated Peter Miller. One day while walking down the street, Whitman approached him and spat in his face. Miller forgave him and moved on. But the innkeeper continued to taunt and humiliate him.

One wintry evening, two men stopped at Whitman's hotel for supper and lodging for the night. Unknown to Whitman, they were spies. When the outspoken innkeeper began to condemn the American cause, the spies jumped up and arrested Whitman for treason. Whitman escaped, but was later captured and taken to Philadelphia for trial.

Word soon reached Miller that Whitman was to be hanged. How would you have felt if you were Miller?

Here's how Peter Miller felt. He thought he saw some redeeming quality in Michael Whitman. So he set out on foot through the snow to visit General George Washington at Valley Forge to intercede for Whitman's life. He pled earnestly on behalf of the traitor, but in vain. "No, Peter," said Washington, "I can't grant you the life of your friend. I intend to make an example of him."

"Friend?" said Miller. "Friend? Why, Michael Whitman is my worst enemy! He taunts and reviles me without end, but I am commanded by my Lord to bless those that persecute me."

Washington was touched and astonished. "You mean you walked more than 60 miles through the snow to save the life of your worst enemy? Well, that puts the matter in a different light. I'll grant your request. But you must deliver the pardon yourself."

Washington signed the pardon and handed it to Miller, who at once set out for West Chester, 15 miles from Valley Forge, where the execution was to take place that same afternoon. He arrived just as Whitman was being escorted to the scaffold. Upon seeing him, Whitman scoffed, "There's 'Old Man Miller.' He has walked all the way from Ephrata to have his revenge gratified today in seeing me hung."

The words were scarcely spoken when Miller, waving the pardon, cried to the executioners: "Halt! I have a stay of execution." Whitman's life was spared, and Peter Miller took Michael Whitman back with him to Ephrata, no longer an enemy, but a friend!

Now what was it that made Peter Miller an effective intercessor? Was it his natural eloquence? No. Was it his friendship with George Washington? Not really. Was it his friendship with Michael Whitman? No. It was his sacrifice. It was the price he paid.

We have intercessors today—lots of them—in government, who speak to legislators on behalf of certain industries. We call them lobbyists. But they do not enjoy a very high reputation, because they are well paid for what they do. They make no sacrifice.

On the same ship that brought John Wesley to America was a Swiss boy from Zurich. The father and mother of the lad both died on the voyage and were buried at sea, and he stepped off the gangway alone, a stranger in a strange land. His name was Abraham Bininger. One day, after he had grown to manhood, he asked to be sent to tell the story of the cross to the slaves on the island of St. Thomas, having heard of their great misery and degradation.

When he arrived at the island, he learned that it was against the law for any person but a slave to preach to the slaves. It was the policy of the planters to keep the Blacks in ignorance and superstition. So Abraham thought and prayed.

Pretty soon the governor of St. Thomas received a letter from Abraham. In the letter the writer begged urgently to be allowed to become a slave for the rest of his life, promising to serve as a slave faithfully, provided he could give his leisure time to preaching to his fellow slaves.

The governor sent the letter to the king of Denmark, who was so touched by it that he sent an edict empowering Abraham Bininger to tell the story of the gospel when and wherever he chose—to Black or White, bond or free.

Now why was Bininger such a successful advocate for the slaves? Because of his sacrifice.

Carl Wilkins and Eric Guttschuss work for ADRA, the Adventist Development and Relief Organization, a charitable organization which goes in harm's way, not with a gun, but with a helping hand.

One day the two men were driving through the deceptively green hills of Rwanda, recently baptized by blood when the Hutus attempted to exterminate the Tutsis. The two were headed for an orphanage in a nearby town, when they spotted a hitchhiker along the road and stopped to pick her up.

As Carl and Eric bumped over the potholed road, they noticed on the forehead of their passenger a deep scar. There was another on the back of her head. Carl asked if there was a story behind those scars. She answered in her native language, with the help of a local pastor who interpreted for her.

Carl and Eric listened with awe to her shocking testimony. During the recent bloodbath, when entire churches full of people were hacked to death, a man had attacked her. He killed her husband, who was a pastor, and he left her for dead, with machete slashes across her face and head. But after the attackers had left, her son came from his hiding place and rescued her, saving her life.

With great emotion she continued. "During the terrible slayings I saw the man who killed my husband and wounded me. He had once been a member of my husband's congregation. Of course, the man did not know that I was not dead when he walked away."

Months later this woman went shopping in a busy, crowded outdoor marketplace, and came face-to-face with this very man whose treachery had caused her such pain. They each stood still, staring at each other for a moment, unable to move. The man was transfixed by her horrible scars. He was sure he had killed her in the fury of the massacre.

Her tormenter began to tremble. Others in the market became aware and watched to see what would happen as perspiration continued to roll down the criminal's face and chest. "Why is he acting like this?" they asked. "What is wrong with this man?"

Turning to them, the pastor's wife said calmly, "This man saw me in the hospital when I was very sick, and he did not think I was going to live. That is why he is so surprised to see me today."

Then she walked up to the man and spoke his name, saying, "Come with me."

She took him to her home and exchanged his sweat-drenched shirt for a clean one from her own son's closet. Then she said words that must have been the hardest words she'd ever spoken: "I don't know what else you have done or who else might accuse you, but as for me, I forgive you."

And then he left. She had lost track of him. But now, she said, she goes from house to house selling books that tell the good news of God's love and forgiveness.

It was Eric Guttschuss who published this story in the *Adventist Review,* January 8, 1998. He writes, "As Carl and I took the woman to her small house in the nearby town, I knew something inside me had changed. Her story of the ultimate forgiveness would remain with me forever. I still see her scars when I close my eyes really tight."

Only God knows her name. She has no idea how much good she has done. By forgiving her trespasser, she has made many whole—including thousands she will never meet this side of heaven. Her sacrifice sets us aglow with grace. Just as the tiny coin given by the poor widow that Jesus commended has resulted in a Niagara of riches flowing to support the gospel, so this story of forgiveness will provide new healing and hope to hurting hearts seared with the poison of resentment and bitterness.

But the sacrifice of Bininger, and Peter Miller, and the widow from Rwanda can't hold a candle to the sacrifice of Jesus Christ.

Jesus gave up more and won more. He laid aside the crown and the glory and came down, down, deep down into the darkness and filth of human depravity. And there He humbled Himself, even to the cross. He was made to be sin for us. There He paid the price for our sins. He died the death we deserve that we might have the life He deserves.

When human beings incurred a debt we could not pay, our Creator took responsibility for us and paid the debt. The traditional term for this is vicarious substitutionary atonement. Today this concept has been questioned even in certain Adventist circles.

After all, isn't it unfair to punish one person for the sin of another? And how does the mediation or intercession of Jesus make sense? If God is loving, why does Jesus need to argue with Him to get Him to forgive us?

Why is God such a meany?

I was once riding a bus on a class trip when I was falsely accused by a teacher of throwing a spitball and moved to another seat. That rankled. How unfair! To bear the shame of another's crime! But then I was just a teenager, and I didn't volunteer to be the victim. And I bore no relationship to the perpetrator. And I was hardly innocent on other counts.

But Jesus is not some randomly chosen created being; He is the Creator, and bears the same relationship to the race that a father does to a child. And parents make atonement for their children *all the time!* Anyone who has ever watched a television court program knows that whenever minor children commit an offense—say, damage someone's car—the parents pay. Why? Because the children don't have the resources. So vicarious atonement makes sense even from the standpoint of twentieth century jurisprudence.

Suppose a child breaks a vase in a store, and the parent says, "Put it on my bill." No store owner would say, "Oh no, that would be unjust and unfair! The one who did the damage must pay." But the child cannot afford to pay, so someone else must pay on his or her behalf. The idea of vicarious atonement is an everyday part of our culture.

Here is another way of looking at the matter. Second Corinthians 5:14 says, "One died for all, and therefore all died." Suppose a card is inserted in a book. Then whatever happens to the book happens to the card. If the book is thrown into the fire, or into the water, the card goes with it.

Now Paul's most common expression in the New Testament is "in Christ." Whatever can this mean? It means that once we are incorporated into Christ, then what happens to Him happens to us. When He died, we died. When He rose, we rose with Him.

And now that He is in heaven at God's right hand, interceding for us, we are seated in heavenly places up there with Him (Eph. 2:6). This is great news, but it introduces a new perplexity.

Why does Jesus have to intercede for us with God at all? Doesn't God love us too? Is God an old meany who has to be cajoled into compassion by a merciful Jesus?

It has become common lately to point out that God does not need someone to convince Him to be nice to us. This is true in the sense that God is the one who originated the plan of salvation and sent Jesus to die, so He obviously has compassion for the fallen. But have you ever noticed that whenever the God of the Old Testament (who is also the God of the New) gets into a discussion with someone over the issue of how to deal with some offending group, God is almost always arguing for justice, while His human sparring partner argues for mercy?

Think about it. In Genesis 18 Abraham begs God to spare the city of Sodom if only 10 righteous people can be found there.

In Job 42:7-10 God is angry with Eliphaz and his two friends, who had not told the truth about Him, and He accepts their sacrifice only after Job prays for them.

When God and Moses argued, God wanted to destroy his perverse parishioners, but Moses argued for pardon, and God granted his request (Num. 14:19, 20). Later Moses obtained forgiveness for Aaron (Deut. 9:20).

Hezekiah obtains healing and forgiveness for his people in 2 Chronicles 30:18-20.

God threatened to bring swarms of locusts upon Israel in Amos 7:1-3, but the prophet Amos cried out, "Sovereign Lord, forgive! How can Jacob survive? He is so small!" So the Lord relented. "This will not happen," the Lord said.

All of these intercessors obtained mercy for others by arguing against divine justice.

Now if God is so kind and loving, then why does He seem to have a bias toward retribution? I wish we could say that God is merely pretending, but sometimes, as in the case of Sodom and the Flood, not to mention the fire at the end of the world, the argument for mercy fails, and God brings actual retribution. Jesus is not just playacting as an intercessor, but is actually restraining the avenging hand of God.

Now that has kind of a harsh sound, doesn't it? This is a problem for some. Didn't Jesus say that He and the Father are One? Was He lying? Is the Godhead schizophrenic?

Some things can best be understood by analogy. In America we have a system of justice in which some members of the court argue for punishment, while others argue for leniency. The court will have a prosecutor, and at the same time appoint a public defender for the accused. They argue with each other. Yet they may even be paid out of the same office. Is the court schizophrenic? Is this a weakness of the system? No, it's a strength! It's all part of a well-functioning system of justice.

Let's look at what happens from time to time in a normal, well-adjusted, happy family. The child breaks the rules. Dad gets upset. Dad and Mom sit down to talk it over. Dad is pacing back and forth and saying, "That girl has got to be punished!" So what does Mom say? "Oh honey, don't be too hard on her." Sometimes it works the other way around.

Now which of them is right?   Which of them love the child more?

Well, something like that is true among the members of the Godhead. There is a part of God which always seeks justice, and another part which loves mercy. And while sinners always root for mercy for themselves, others are rooting for justice. You see—and this is a key point—there are other creatures in the universe that have never sinned. We sinners have a bias toward mercy. But sinless beings, such as unfallen angels, have a bias toward justice. It's not just our welfare that God has to think about, but also the rights and the feelings of all His unfallen creatures, who have reason to wonder why God has put up with sinners for so long.

Let's look at the problem through their eyes, something we normally never do. Getting into their head requires a little thought experiment. I am going to use a rather vivid illustration which may be emotionally wrenching.

Suppose your best friend has a beautiful young daughter. One day she is abducted, raped, and stabbed to death. The murderer is caught and brought to trial. Turns out he has done this before. Sitting in the courtroom, you listen with increasing rage as the brilliant defense attorney argues that his client, the murderer, had a disadvantaged childhood and ought to be set free. You can hardly control yourself as the judge turns to the accused and asks,

"Are you sorry for what you did?"

"Yes."

"Do you promise never to do it again?"

"Yes."

"All right," declares the judge. "You're free to go."

Would you consider this a shining example of mercy, or a horrible miscarriage of justice? Were you hoping that the judge would let the murderer go free, or were you hoping he would lock him up and throw away the key?

Why are you such a meany?

Get the point? Even if your friend who lost a daughter finds it in his heart to forgive the murderer, the courts of justice of the land still have an obligation to bring retribution. When God forbids Christians to take vengeance, but to leave that to Him (Rom. 12:19), He is only saying "Don't take the law into your own hands," a rule of every advanced society. But the rule works only if there are courts of justice to stand behind it. If there is no official punishment, no judicial vengeance, then the rule of law breaks down and it's every man for himself.

So the Judge of the universe has to be fair to all sides. When He punishes the guilty, it is not out of malice, but out of a love for justice. Inequities must be balanced. Someone must pay. God cannot, like the unjust judge above, just let bygones be bygones.

Yet even as God stands for justice, another part of Him longs for mercy. So long ago God took upon Himself the task of reconciling justice and mercy by absorbing into His own person the retribution of the broken law. He sent His beloved Son to die. He did this because—wonder of wonders—He loves sinners as much as He loves His own Son!

Jesus told His disciples that God Himself loved them.

Until now you have not asked for anything in my name. Ask and you will receive, and your joy will be complete. . . . In that day you will ask in my name. I am not saying that I will ask the Father on your behalf. No, the Father himself loves you because you have loved me and have believed that I came from God (John 16:24-27).

Jesus is talking to His faithful disciples, minus Judas, after the Lord's Supper and just before His crucifixion. He has already interceded for them many times in all-night prayer sessions. Remember what he told Peter: "I have prayed for you, Simon, that your faith may not fail" (Luke 22:32). And He is about to intercede for them again in a few moments: "I pray for them. I am not praying for the world, but for those you have given me, for they are yours" (John 17:9). So Jesus is clearly not saying, "I will never again ask the Father on your behalf." And He certainly is not saying that from now on they can come to God directly, because a few moments earlier Jesus said, "No one comes to the Father except through me" (John 14:6). In fact, He reminds them, over and over again, that whenever they ask God for a favor, they must ask in His name, not in their own (John 16:23, 24, 26).

So when Jesus says "I am not saying that I will ask the Father on your behalf. No, the Father himself loves you," He is paying them a compliment and building them up for the trial they are about to face. He is reassuring them that God is on their side even in His absence. *After all, during those hours He is lying in the tomb they will be without an intercessor.* Yet they are safe, because the Father Himself loves them. Jesus has already put in a good word for them.

And that is what Jesus has done for all of those who have accepted Him as their Savior. He puts in a good word for us. He asks that the favor due to Him be extended to us, even when we make mistakes. First John 2:1 puts it this way: "If anybody does sin, we have one who speaks to the Father in our defense—Jesus Christ, the Righteous One." Notice that the text doesn't say that if we are good, Jesus speaks to the Father in our defense. No, it's when we have sinned that we really need a defender. And the reason we continue to need Him is because we continue to sin. Fortunately, after what Jesus went through for us on Calvary, God just can't say no to His Son!

And that is why we pray in Jesus' name, and wear the clothes He provides for us. Our lives are polluted with sin, and we are offensive to a holy God—

just as a pet dog who has been out rolling in dung is offensive to us. We can't just bring our pollution into the throne room of heaven any more than we would be granted an audience with an earthly king while wearing muddy shoes and filthy clothing. But when we wash our robes, coming to God in Jesus' name, that name opens the portals of heaven to us.

So here, then, is the good news: We have a friend in the court of heaven. Jesus is God's go-between. As long as we are still committing new sins, we still need new intercession. And our Intercessor "is able to save completely those who come to God through him, because he always lives to intercede for them" (Hebrews 7:25).

So if someone wonders what record of human achievements we would launch into space to be discovered one day by some transgalactic civilization, we can do better than Bach. As Bach is to music, so Jesus is to Bach. Intergalactic billboards are not needed. Jesus is our billboard, already in heaven interceding for us. And as if that were not enough, Romans says the Holy Spirit intercedes for us too! We have Friends in high places. And He wants to make beautiful music in us.

"For Christ did not enter a man-made sanctuary that was only a copy of the true one; he entered heaven itself, now to appear for us in God's presence" (Heb. 9:24). "And if any man sin, we have an advocate with the Father, Jesus Christ the righteous" (1 John 2:1, KJV).

CHAPTER 12

Never Give Up

A few years ago there was an interesting article in the Wall Street Journal about a fellow by the name of Jay Walker. That year Mr. Walker hit the big time. He became a billionaire. He founded Priceline.com, a company on the Internet where you can pick your own price for airline tickets, and it went public in the spring of 1999, achieving a stock value of over 10 billion dollars.

But what interested me most were the business schemes of Mr. Walker that failed. He tried selling retailer's catalogs through bookstores. It was a disaster. He launched his own newspaper in Ithaca, New York. It folded. Then he put together a think tank for ideas for new businesses on the Internet. Eventually they came up with Priceline.com.

I've been thinking about this little tale and I've come up with a question for you: have you failed enough?

I'm not talking about intentional failure, of course; I'm talking about trying and failing and trying and failing over and over until you succeed.

Most of us haven't, you see. We're so afraid of failure that we never muddle our way through to the big success. Turns out that the most successful people are generally the ones who have failed the most. Success usually lies on the far side of failure.

Take Walt Disney for example. He was fired by a newspaper because—now get this—he lacked ideas! After that first failure he proceeded to go bankrupt several times before he finally built the Magic Kingdom.

Babe Ruth struck out 1,330 times. Of course, he also hit 714 home runs. But for every home run, he struck out twice.

R. H. Macy failed seven times before his store in New York caught on.

I have some friends who are writers. Being a writer sounds kind of glamorous, doesn't it? Actually it's a lot of hard work. How do you get to be a writer? One definition holds that you are an honest-to-goodness writer once you have accumulated 200 rejection slips. You can't call yourself a writer until you've failed enough.

But what would you call English novelist John Creasey? He accumulated 753 rejection slips. Then he published 564 books.

Perhaps you have read one of the *Chicken Soup for the Soul* series. You may not know that the original manuscript was rejected by 80 publishers. There's no market for it, wise editors said. But the poor authors didn't have the good sense to give up. Since no publisher would take it, they had to publish it themselves. It made them millions.

So I've been thinking about failure lately. And one verse in particular keeps coming to mind. It's found in Proverbs 24:16, "Though a righteous man falls seven times, he rises again, but the wicked are brought down by calamity."

Now you might expect something more like this: "The wicked man falls seven times, but the righteous man stands upright." But no, that's not what it says. God says that a righteous person falls seven times, but every time he falls, he gets back up, dusts himself off, and presses on toward the goal. That, my friend, is the secret of success—financial, social, or spiritual.

Richard Edler wrote a book called *If I Knew Then What I Know Now*. In it he asks a number of CEOs and other leaders to share the most important lesson they learned from life, something they wished they had known 25 years ago. I want to share two of those answers with you.

Here's what Bill Lipien, CEO of Mitchum, Jones & Templeton, considered to be his most important lesson: "Expect to fail miserably 30% of the time."

J. Melvin Muse, CEO of Muse Cordero Chen, offers this piece of advice: "Make lots of mistakes. Mistakes are the fuel for fast career development. Learn how to make brilliant recoveries. And then never make the same mistake twice. Do this and your career will move faster toward the top than your more conservative associates'."

Success lies on the other side of failure. You have to go through failure to success. Really big successes come only after repeated failure.

Fear of failure is one of our most disabling fears. It's an ego problem. Failure didn't use to bother us so much. How many times did we fail before learning to walk? Before riding a bike? Before we could swim? Or dive? Or hit a home run?

James and Jerrilyn are, let's say, parents of a perfectly normal toddler. Their little bundle of potentiality begins to take her first steps, only to fall down again and again. James and Jerri watch her progress at first with delight, and then with increasing dismay. Finally they decide to keep a record. Each fall is registered with another stroke on the whiteboard. At last the fearful, tearful parents can endure no more. After their little one succumbs to gravity for the fiftieth time, the merciful parents resolve to put an end to her sad litany of failure. Learning to walk is simply too hard. So they tie her feet together to keep her safely on the floor.

Absurd nonsense. Well, God doesn't do that either. But the real point is *everyone who keeps on trying eventually learns to walk*. The infant is not smart enough to give up. So he or she never does.

Some really advanced walkers even go further and learn to ski or skateboard. (Others, like myself, being of less agile persuasion, never make it that far.)

Thomas Edison might be regarded as one of the world's greatest failures. Here is a man who tried over a thousand different light bulbs until he got it right. Have you ever failed at something a thousand times before you got it right? If you had, your name might be right up there with that of Thomas Edison.

Actually Edison didn't think of these failed experiments as failures. He regarded them as steps in a long process. But late in his life something happened to Thomas that would have defeated a lesser man.

Thomas Edison's son Charles, one-time governor of New Jersey, tells the story. On the night of December 9, 1914, Edison Industries was virtually destroyed by fire. Edison lost 2 million dollars that night and much of his life's work went up in flames. He was insured for only $238,000, because the buildings had been made of concrete, at that time thought to be fireproof.

Charles was 24, Thomas was 67. The young man ran about frantically, trying to find his father. Finally he came upon him, standing near the fire, his face ruddy in the glow, his white hair blown by the December winds.

"My heart ached for him," Charles Edison said. "He was 67—no longer a young man—and everything was going up in flames. He spotted me.

"Charles," he shouted, "where's your mother?"

"I don't know, Dad," I said.

"Find her. Bring her here. She will never see anything like this again as long as she lives."

The next morning, walking about the charred embers of all his hopes and dreams, Thomas Edison said, "There is great value in disaster. All our mistakes are burned up. Thank God we can start anew."

Three weeks after the fire, his firm delivered the first phonograph.

The principle of Proverbs 24:16, always getting up when you fall, works on many levels. Victory goes to the one who perseveres, both here and hereafter. Luke 8:15 speaks of the good seed from the hand of the sower representing "those with a noble and good heart, who hear the word, retain it, and by persevering produce a crop." Hebrews 10:36 tells us to "persevere so that when you have done the will of God, you will receive what he has promised." James 1:12 counsels, "Blessed is the man who perseveres under trial, because when he has stood the test, he will receive the crown of life that God has promised to those who love him." The same idea is found in Romans 2:7, "To those who by persistence in doing good seek glory, honor and immortality, he will give eternal life." Everyone who keeps on keeping on, no matter how many times they might fall down in the process, will find their feet walking on streets of gold.

Don't misunderstand. Perserverance in good works is never a ground or basis of our salvation. The ground of our salvation is the doing and dying of Jesus Christ. It is, however, a condition. We can never be saved by good works; and we can never be saved without them. The New Testament teaches that we are saved

if we abide in Christ's word (John 8:31)

if we suffer with Christ (Rom. 8:17)

if we continue in God's kindness (Rom. 11:22)

if we hold firmly to the apostles' word (1 Cor. 15:2)

if we do not grow weary (Gal. 6:9)

if we continue in the faith (Col. 1:23)

if we persevere (1 Tim. 4:16)

if we endure, and do not deny Him (2 Tim. 2:12; Matt. 10:32, 33)

if we hold fast our confidence firmly unto the end (Heb. 3:6, 12-14)

if we have endurance and do not shrink back (Heb. 10:35-39)

if what we have heard abides in us (1 John 2:24)

These are all conditions. Salvation is clearly conditional upon our perseverance (cp. Mark 13:13; Rom. 2:7; James 1:12; 2 Peter 1:5-11; Rev. 2:10, 11, 26).

No trait is more important to success—certainly not talent, intelligence, or ability—than perseverance, in this life or the next. "We consider blessed those who have persevered. You have heard of Job's perseverance and have seen what the Lord finally brought about" (James 5:11). Jesus in Revelation 2:3 blesses "you [who] have persevered and have endured hardships for my name, and have not grown weary."

So never give up.

When he was a little boy the other children called him "Sparky," after a comic strip horse named Sparkplug. Sparky never did shake that nickname. School was all but impossible for Sparky. He failed every single subject in the eighth grade. In high school he distinguished himself as the worst physics student in his school's history. He also flunked Latin, algebra, and English. He was poor in sports, and socially awkward. In high school Sparky never once asked a girl out. He was too afraid of being turned down.

Sparky was a loser. He knew it, and his classmates knew it. His one and only skill was drawing. He was proud of his own art work. Of course, no one else appreciated it. When he submitted some cartoons to the editors of his senior high class yearbook, they were rejected.

Nevertheless, Sparky determined on a career as a professional artist. He applied to Walt Disney studios. He half expected to be rejected.

And sure enough, he was.

But Sparky never gave up. He wrote his autobiography in cartoons. He described his childhood self, the little boy loser, the chronic underachiever, in a cartoon character the whole world now knows. "Sparky" Charles Monroe Schulz created the "Peanuts" comic strip and the little cartoon boy whose kite would never fly—Charlie Brown.

You see, you just can't get a good man down. Or a good woman. Take my wife, for example. She's never given up on me, no matter how many times her plan of reform has failed (she has made some progress). God hasn't given up on me either. And He certainly hasn't given up on you.

So never give up on yourself.

Sir Winston Churchill, aging and sickly, was once asked to give the commencement address at Oxford University. He gave perhaps the shortest commencement speech of all time.

The man who had almost single-handedly inspired and cajoled England to enter, to endure, and to win the war against Hitler tottered to the podium. Hanging his cane on the desk, he peered at his young audience through his thick, bushy eyebrows, set his famous jaw, and exclaimed, "Never give up!"

He took a step backward and surveyed those eager young faces once again. Reaching into some great, inner reservoir, Sir Winston's legendary voice rose in intensity, "Never give up!"

After an extra long pause, he roared, "Never give up!"

Then, he took his cane and shuffled back to his seat. Stunned, the graduates sat in silence. Then the applause began and ended in a thunderous, standing ovation.

I suspect that struggling Christians that keep rising whenever they fall attract a large audience of invisible onlookers. A crowd of angels must collect around those dogged persisters, those plodding Christians that never give up. We may not be able to hear heaven's cheerleaders and their anthems now. But someday . . .

From the 1992 Summer Olympics in Barcelona comes a beautiful story of triumph over failure; of falling and rising again. No one remembers the runner who came in first that day. The runner we remember is Derek Redmond, a sprinter from Britain. Derek ran in the men's 400-meter semifinals. This was a vindication of sorts. Four years earlier, in Seoul, Korea, just minutes before running the 400, he had pulled his Achilles tendon on the warm-up track, so he couldn't run. Now life was offering him another chance.

The guns sounded and the runners were off. But only 150 meters into the race Derek's hamstring popped and he fell to the ground in agony. Officials ran onto the track with a stretcher. He waved them off, struggled to his feet and began hopping, inches at a time, down the track.

Suddenly a man leaped out of the stands over the railing onto the track, ran to Derek's side and threw his arm around him. Together they hobbled the last 100 meters to the end. It was Derek's father, Jim Redmond. He had sacrificed much to get his son to the games. Five minutes later father and son walked across the finish line, and 60,000 people gave them a standing ovation.

When asked about it later, his father said, "We had an agreement he was going to finish the race. This is his last Olympics. He trained eight years for this day. I wasn't going to let him not finish."

That is what our heavenly Father does for us. We are all stumbling toward the mark of the high calling of Jesus Christ. It's two steps forward, one step back. We are all disabled in some way. But the secret to victory is never staying down. Jesus is there beside us, helping us up, leading us onward and forward to victory.

"Though a righteous man falls seven times, he rises again." So never give up. Angels are watching you. All heaven is rooting for you. And your heavenly Father is waiting to wrap His arms around you and walk beside you to the finish line. Commit your life to Him and resolve that you will keep on keeping on, and trust that He will see you through to the end.

CHAPTER 13

The Gleam in the Eye of God

I once saw hanging on an office wall a picture of Abraham Lincoln that had obviously been created by a computer. It was composed of thousands of much smaller pictures. You've probably seen it. Each line and shadow on the face of Lincoln was the result of a clever arrangement of tiny reproductions of thousands of photographs taken during the Civil War. I noticed one detail in particular. As I looked closely at the gleam in Lincoln's left eye, it turned out to be a tiny portrait of the head of a man.

Now that got me to thinking. Suppose you could look upon a portrait of the face of God. What would you see in His eyes? If you looked closely enough, I think you would see a gleam in the eye of God. Then if you looked even closer, you would discover that gleam in the eye of God was you! David the shepherd understood this. In Psalm 17:8 he prayed this prayer to God: "Keep me as the apple [pupil] of your eye."

There is a saying, "before you were even a gleam in the eye of your parents." But there never was a time when you weren't a gleam in God's eye. And if even the gleams in human eyes can turn into a live baby, then think of the potential of being a gleam in God's eye!

Maybe you're thinking, *Not me. I'm not the gleam in God's eye! I'm just the lint on His shoulder.* Well, even if that were true, it still makes you part of the picture. Each of us has a bit part to play in God's plan. We cannot understand the plan, but we find fulfillment by playing our part. When we commit our lives to God, He plugs us into His grand scheme. We discover our place in the world. We become part of the picture. A bonsai in His garden.

You may have a hard time believing that diamond-like gleam in God's eye is you. Maybe you feel more like a piece of coal. Or maybe you're just a nut, and you're getting stepped on, and life is crushing you into something like peanut butter. No diamond here, just a big gooey mess.

Did you know that scientists can make diamonds out of peanut butter? A few years ago the Discovery Channel did a feature on it. No kidding. All it takes is the right equipment. The scientists put the peanut butter into a small container and put the container in the middle of a large machine which applied incredible pressure, which in turn generated a great deal of heat, and when it was all over they took out a dark mass, and in the middle of it was a diamond. It wasn't gem quality, but it was indeed a diamond. They used peanut butter just to show that anything that contains a large amount of carbon can be turned into diamond with the proper amount of pressure and heat.

In fact you can make diamonds from tequila, which is a far better use for that beverage than the traditional one. There is even a commercial firm now that will turn the ashes of your loved one into a diamond. It's quite expensive, but if you supply them with cremated remains, they will create a real diamond out of those ashes.

If human beings can do that, just think what God can do! Don't look now, but God is making diamonds out of ashes. He still does it today, just like He did for 11 disciples soon after the darkest day of their lives.

Few people have ever known such total destruction of all hopes and ambitions, such despair for the future, as those 11 men who kept the darkest Sabbath of their lives nineteen and a half centuries ago. Their hopes lay buried in the tomb with Jesus of Nazareth, the one they had placed their trust in as God's Messiah. They had watched in horror as His gentle hands were nailed to a cross. Now He was gone. And they were destitute. The magnificent dreams they cherished had turned to ashes.

God was about to turn their ashes into diamonds.

During His lifetime He was little appreciated even by his own family. He didn't have the best educational credentials, and so he made his living as a day laborer. One day he decided on a career change, left his job, and achieved a measure of fame as an itinerant preacher. His brothers didn't have a very high opinion of him. They thought he was unbalanced, and at one point tried to take him into custody (see Mark 3:21, 31). His peculiar ideas annoyed the local authorities. Eventually he said some things that turned the crowd against him (John 6:66). He was eventually arrested, tried, and convicted of treason (Mark 15:2, 26). He was finally executed as a common criminal by the cruelest method possible.

His life and death changed the course of human history. More books have been written about Jesus, and more songs sung, than about anyone else who ever lived, making Him the most influential figure of all time. Today He's the hope of the human race, the all-time, undisputed, undefeated champion of love. And all because He did something no one ever did before: He rose again from the grave.

Now the risen Jesus has planted a garden. He spends lots of time in His garden. He dotes on the beautiful specimens he has there. One of them is you. You are his bonsai.

Here's what you need to remember about bonsai: they are not redwoods. They're not even white pines. They're not straight. They tend to be crooked. In fact, the rule among bonsai growers seems to be, "If it's not bent, bend it." That's what gives them beauty and character.

If life has left you bent and broken, you surely aren't feeling like a work of art. It's hard to believe you can be among the chosen when life seems to have left you on the sidelines. Have you ever felt like you were stranded in the middle of a lake without a paddle, and a storm is coming, and there is a hole in your canoe? Do you feel like as Charlie Brown is to sports, so you are to faith? Do you feel like someone is always jerking the ball away when you go to kick that field goal in the game of life?

Well be patient. God is not finished with you yet. You are His pet project. He's just getting started. A bonsai takes time. Let Him cut and bend a little. Put in the prayer time and the practice time and the study time and let God do the transforming.

Just don't steal from yourself by refusing to spend time with God.

Zig Ziglar tells the story of three thieves. The name of the first thief was Emanuel Nenger. The year is 1887. The scene is a small neighborhood grocery store. A middle-aged gentleman is in the store buying some turnip greens. He gives the clerk a $20 bill and she starts to put the $20 bill in the cash drawer to give him his change. Then the clerk looks down at her fingers and she notices some of the ink from the $20 bill is coming off on her fingers, which are wet because she's been wrapping those turnip greens. And she looked up at Mr. Nenger. Here's a man she's known for years. She looks down at the $20 bill. She's shocked. She wonders to herself, "Is this man giving me a counterfeit $20 bill?" And then she discounts it almost immediately because Emanuel Nenger is an old and trusted friend. So she says, "No, he wouldn't do that." So she gives him his change and he goes on his way.

But $20 is an awful lot of money in 1887 and so she decides to contact the police. They get a search warrant; they look through Emanuel Nenger's home. Up in his attic they find the facilities for reproducing $20 bills. The facilities are rather simple. It's an artist's easel and the paint brushes and the paints, because Emanuel Nenger is laboriously, stroke by stroke, hand-painting those $20 bills. You see, he was in fact, a master artist. And while they were up there they found three portraits that Emanuel Nenger had painted. They sold those portraits at public auction for a little over $16,000. That's over $5,000 per portrait. But here's the irony—it took him almost the same length of time to paint a $20 bill that it took him to paint a $5,000 portrait. Emanuel Nenger was a thief who was stealing from himself. Anytime we try to take the shortcuts, anytime we put trash into our bodies or into our minds, anytime we do something we wouldn't want published on the front page of the newspaper, we are stealing from ourselves.

The second thief was a man who really made a lot of history back in the Roaring Twenties. Arthur Berry was a jewel thief, and a good one. He also was a snob. Arthur Berry would not steal from just anybody; oh no, you had to have your name in the upper echelons of the society pages in order for Arthur Berry to come calling. As a matter of fact, the women of Boston rather boastfully would announce to the world when Arthur Berry had made a social call and stolen their diamonds.

But the police, rather obviously, did not view Arthur Berry in the same light. They were after him hot and heavy. And one night they caught him in the act, shot him three times, he fell through a glass window with three bullets in his body, splinters of glass in his eyes, lying there in excruciating pain, he said, "I ain't goin' to do this anymore!"

He made good his escape and lived outside the penitentiary for a couple of more years, then a jealous woman turned him in and he went to the federal pen for 18 years. When he came out he kept his promise—he did not go back to the life of a jewel thief. He settled in a small New England town, became a respected citizen, and in fact they elected him the commander of a local veteran's organization.

But the word leaked out, and it became known that Arthur Berry, the famous jewel thief, was there, and reporters gathered from all over America to interview this famous jewel thief. And they asked him the customary questions. And finally a young reporter asked him the most poignant question of them all, when he said, "Mr. Berry, you stole from an awful lot of wealthy people in your life as a jewel thief. Let me ask you a question, "From whom did you steal the most?"

And Arthur Berry, without a moment's hesitation said, "That's the easiest question I've ever been asked. The man from whom I stole the most was Arthur Berry. You see, I could have been a baron on Wall Street. I could have been a successful businessman, had I utilized my God-given talents and developed them legitimately. I could have made it big in business but I spent more than two-thirds of my adult life behind bars."

The third thief is you. If you are not spending time with God in prayer, if you are not using the inherent ability that God gave you, if you are not walking in the path of loving service, you are stealing from yourself.

Why not abandon yourself to God? Let Him make something special of your life. Put on Jesus Christ every morning, and ask Him to give you something to do for Him. Don't squander those opportunities. One of the greatest regrets in life is squandered opportunity.

Otto Schindler was a rich industrialist. The opportunity fell into his lap to save the lives of over a thousand of the Jews who worked for him during World War II. It would cost him a fortune. The story is told in the film *Schindler's List*. The emotional climax of the film comes just before the end. Schindler has to flee because the Americans are arresting all Nazis and he is still technically a Nazi. After he says goodbye to the Jews whose lives he saved, just before he drives off, he pulls out a ring his Jewish workers had given him as a token of their gratitude. They had taken the gold out of a worker's gold dental bridge and melted it down into a ring, engraved with a Talmudic quotation, "Whoever saves one life saves the world entire." When they gave it to him Schindler was touched but deeply ashamed. Now he pulls it out of his pocket and says, "It's gold. I could have sold it. . . . I could have saved *one more!*" The one thing he regretted was the one thing he kept for himself. If only he had known then, when he thought he was rich, what he knew now.

You know, you may discover that you don't fit in the choir. Maybe you're like the guy who majored in English, went to work at a steel factory, and ended up as an world-class artist in steel. He pursued his passion and decided to do what he loved best. Don't let them make you a tall, straight white pine if you are called to be a bent-but-beautiful bonsai.

If you're coasting, you're not growing. Don't settle for being limestone if you can be calcite. Don't settle for calcite if you can be quartz. Don't settle for quartz if you can be diamond. Be the best you can be for Jesus.

They say a diamond is forever. But it isn't. Not even the sun is forever. But you are. One of my favorite verses is Daniel 12:3: "Those who are wise will shine like the brightness of the heavens, and those who lead many to righteousness, like the stars for ever and ever." That means that God has a wonderful future in store for you. Long after the sun has burned to ashes you and I will still be shining stars gleaming in the eye of God.

Let's do one last thought experiment. The greatest Coach in the world comes to you and says, "I've been watching you, and I want you on my team. I'm gonna make you a champion. Four years from now we're going all the way to the world competition in the Olympics, and I plan for you to take the gold medal on the uneven parallel bars. Are you in?"

You reply, "You must be dreaming. Sometimes I can't even keep my balance on level ground. I'm the Charlie Brown of acrobatics. There's no way I could ever be that good."

And the Coach replies, "You're right. You're really not that good. Not yet. Not by yourself. But I know a winner when I see one. I'm telling you that you've got what it takes. All you have to do is trust me and do whatever I say.

"It won't be easy. When your friends are out partying, you'll be sweating it out at the gym. You'll fall down a thousand times, sore muscles against the mat. You'll nurse your bruises and then climb back up and try again.

"But one glorious day you'll soar and spin and dance on those bars and leap through thin air like a magic feather, and a million hearts will leap with you. You'll do things no one ever did before. You'll make the impossible look effortless. And when you're done, you'll be a champion forever. And, oh, the shouts and applause and anthems that will fill the air as you stand in the winner's circle to receive the gold! And you will bless the day you met me.

"You were not born to vegetate in front of the television set, or to be enslaved by your addictions, or enervated by your passions. You were created to soar. And I made you for myself. You were my delight. When I made you, all the stars sang for joy. They'll sing again on the day I renew my creation. On that day there will be a kingdom of love and light where nothing sordid, nothing vile, nothing unkind can enter. No fear, no injustice, no pain, no heartache.

"You and Me forever.

"I want you on my team. We're going places, you and I, unimaginable places. Take your fondest dream for yourself and multiply it a thousand times, and it still won't begin to match My dream for you. When I'm through with you, you'll be a creature of such splendor that passing angels will have to veil their eyes.

"You say I'm dreaming. You're right. I'm a dreamer. Please let me make my dream for you come true.

"Come. Follow Me."